THE AGE OF
OBAMA

D1461279

Manchester University Press

THE AGE OF
OBAMA

THE CHANGING PLACE
OF MINORITIES IN BRITISH AND
AMERICAN SOCIETY

Tom Clark, Robert D. Putnam
and Edward Fieldhouse

Drawing on the research of:
David Cutts
Edward Fieldhouse
Robert Ford
Daniel J. Hopkins
Yaojun Li
Ceri Peach
Mary Waters

Manchester University Press
Manchester and New York
distributed in the United States exclusively by Palgrave Macmillan

Published by Manchester University Press
Oxford Road, Manchester M13 9NR, UK
and Room 400, 175 Fifth Avenue, New York, NY 10010, USA
www.manchesteruniversitypress.co.uk

Distributed in the United States exclusively by
Palgrave Macmillan, 175 Fifth Avenue, New York,
NY 10010, USA

Distributed in Canada exclusively by
UBC Press, University of British Columbia, 2029 West Mall,
Vancouver, BC, Canada V6T 1Z2

British Library Cataloguing-in-Publication Data
A catalogue record for this book is available from the British Library

Library of Congress Cataloging-in-Publication Data applied for

ISBN 978 0 7190 8277 1 hardback
ISBN 978 0 7190 8278 8 paperback

First published 2010

Typeset in 11/14pt Minion
by Graphicraft Limited, Hong Kong
Printed in Great Britain
by CPI Antony Rowe Ltd, Chippenham, Wiltshire

Contents

Preface and acknowledgements

A series of comparative academic studies provided the bulk of the raw material for this volume. We thoroughly acknowledge the researchers of these studies, who are listed on the title page. The correspondence between their work and the chapters that follow is not exact, and throughout the text draws on additional sources too. But it is worth acknowledging that Chapter 2 draws particularly heavily on work by Mary Waters; Chapter 3 on work by Ceri Peach; Chapter 4 on work by Yaojun Li; Chapter 5 on work by Edward Fieldhouse and David Cutts; Chapter 6 on the work of Daniel Hopkins; and Chapter 7 on work by Rob Ford. As well as providing our raw material, all these researchers have been generous with their time in responding to our queries throughout the production of this book. Further information on how to access their underlying research is given in the introduction.

The research under-pinning this book is a product of the five-year, £5 million collaboration between the University of Manchester and Harvard, headed by Professor Robert D. Putnam, known as *Social Change: A Harvard-Manchester Initiative* (SCHMI). *The age of Obama* is the first in a series of books examining different aspects of major contemporary social changes, which will include US-UK comparative studies of religion, inequality, and the social impact of changes to the way we work. SCHMI is based at the Institute for Social Change at the University of Manchester, directed by Professor Edward Fieldhouse (www.manchester.ac.uk/socialchange).

The authors gratefully acknowledge the generous funding from the University of Manchester which supports SCHMI and made this book possible. We would especially like to thank the President of the

University of Manchester, Professor Alan Gilbert, and the Dean of the Faculty of Humanities and Vice-President of the University of Manchester, Professor Alistair Ulph, without whom the collaboration would not have been possible. We would also like to thank Tom Sander, Louise Kennedy Converse, Tricia Dennett, Kyle Gibson and Jenny Birchall for their invaluable assistance in organising the SCHMI research programme and summer school on Immigration.

Tables, boxes and figures

Tables

Boxes

Figures

Notes on the authors and contributors

Tom Clark writes editorials for the *Guardian*. Previously, he worked as a special adviser to the British government and an economist at the Institute for Fiscal Studies where he specialised in poverty and welfare.

Robert D. Putnam is Malkin Professor of Public Policy at Harvard University. He established a best-selling audience through his previous books, is active in the media, and engaged with politicians, including American presidents and British prime ministers. *The Economist* hailed his *Making Democracy Work* (1993) as 'a great work of social science, worthy to rank alongside de Tocqueville, Pareto and Weber'. *Prospect* magazine ranked him among the world's top 100 intellectuals in 2009, and his outstanding contribution to scholarship in political science was recognised with the Skytte Prize in 2006.

Edward Fieldhouse is Professor of Social and Political Science at the University of Manchester where he is Director of the Institute for Social Change. He has published on a wide range of issues, including political engagement and participation, voter turnout and voting behaviour, with a particular focus on the interaction between individuals and the local context. He is author of a recent book *Neither Left nor Right? The Liberal Democrats and the Electorate* (2005) with Andrew Russell.

David Cutts is a Research Fellow at the Institute for Social Change, University of Manchester. His research has focused on geographical and contextual effects in voting and attitudes, voter turnout, political engagement and participation and social networks.

Robert Ford is a Post-doctoral Fellow in the Cathie Marsh Centre for Census and Survey Research, University of Manchester. His research has concerned British attitudes towards immigrants and ethnic minorities.

Dan Hopkins is a Post-doctoral Fellow and Lecturer in the Department of Government, Harvard University. He has undertaken research on ethnic and racial diversity, political behaviour, local and urban politics and attitudes on poverty.

Yaojun Li is Professor of Sociology at the Institute for Social Change, University of Manchester. His main interests are in social mobility, social capital and ethnic differences. He has published many papers in top sociology journals, book chapters and research reports for government agencies.

Ceri Peach is part-time Professor in the Institute for Social Change, University of Manchester. Between 1992 and 2007 he was Professor of Social Geography at Oxford. He has held fellowships and visiting professorships at the Australian National University, Yale, Berkeley, UBC Harvard and Princeton. His major research interest is the segregation of ethnic and religious minorities. He has advised the British government on minority segregation, faith communities and Census questions. He was the American Association of Geographers Distinguished Ethnic Geographer of the year in 2008.

Mary C. Waters is M. E. Zukerman Professor of Sociology at Harvard University. Her research interests have included immigration and inter-group relations. Recent books are *Inheriting the City: The Second Generation Comes of Age* (2008) with Jennifer Holdaway, Philip Kasinitz and John Mollenkopf; and *The New Americans: A Guide to Immigration Since 1965* (2007) with Reed Ueda and Helen Marrow.

1

Introduction:
the diversity revolution

I have brothers, sisters, nieces, nephews, uncles and cousins, of every race and every hue, scattered across three continents, and for as long as I live, I will never forget that in no other country on Earth is my story even possible. It's a story that hasn't made me the most conventional candidate. But it is a story that has seared into my genetic makeup the idea that this nation is more than the sum of its parts – that out of many, we are truly one. (Senator Barack Obama, March 2008)

In electing Barack Obama, the United States has not only chosen a leader who embodies the union of black and white America. It has also selected a President who reflects the ties between established Americans and new arrivals. His white Kansan mother married not only a black man, but a man born abroad. There is no denying that Obama has won real power, but does his arrival also reflect wider change in the treatment of America's immigrants and minorities? And if so, are similar changes under way in the UK? Or is it true, as Obama suggests, that his story is a uniquely American one?

These are among the questions that this book seeks to answer, by drawing on sweeping, collaborative research – and particular papers – from a distinguished team from Harvard and Manchester Universities. The work was carried out under the auspices of SCHMI – *Social Change: A Harvard-Manchester Initiative*. A series of five comparative academic studies provides us with the raw material for this volume. We thoroughly acknowledge our debt to the authors of these papers, without which there would be no book. The papers contain more detail on methodology and much greater depth than it is possible to explore in this monograph, so we refer the interested reader to the full underlying analysis which is available on our

website.[1] One data-driven difference between the papers, reflected in
what follows, is worth being explicit about at the outset – namely,
the territorial reach of 'Britain', with Scotland sometimes included
and sometimes not.[2]

Our transatlantic collaboration refreshes long-standing links: Henry
Dunster, who became the first president of Harvard in 1640, came
from the Mancunian hinterland. More importantly, though, it brings
together top academics in two different nations, and so allows us to
get to the bottom of the same searching questions in two different
countries at once.

The diversity revolution

Pardeep Saini was discovered in the undercarriage of a jumbo jet at
Heathrow airport in 1996. During the ten-hour flight from Delhi to
London, temperatures plummeted to −40°, and his brother was killed.
Yet Pardeep somehow survived. On the other side of the Atlantic,
hundreds of people die every year trying to enter the United States
– whether by swimming across the Rio Grande, trudging through
the desert or charting the ocean on home-made boats. But if hundreds die, hundreds of thousands make it. The pull of the rich world

[1] The papers are available at: www.ageofobamabook.com/research.html. As well as the five
comparative papers, we have drawn heavily on the UK-only study by Rob Ford (2008).

[2] The UK comprises England and Wales, Scotland and Northern Ireland; Great Britain
comprises England and Wales and Scotland. Both Northern Ireland and Scotland have their
own census offices and some questions on ethnicity and religion differ from those posed
in England and Wales. The overwhelming majority of the black and minority population
of the UK is located in England and Wales. In what follows, in order to retain the flow
of the text, we contrast 'Britain' and 'the UK' with the US without specifying at every
mention whether Scotland or for that matter Northern Ireland is included. In broad terms,
Chapters 3 and 5 concentrate on England and Wales, which in the latter case reflects the
reach of the Citizenship Survey, and in the former the fact that Scotland and Northern
Ireland code ethnicity differently in the census. The analysis in Chapter 4 is also based on
the census, but includes the whole of Great Britain, adjusting for these differences. Chapter 7
chiefly focuses on Great Britain as a whole (reflecting the reach of the British Social Attitudes
survey), although some of its charts cover the UK as a whole – including Northern Ireland
– reflecting the make-up of the House of Commons. In some of the charts in Chapter 2
Scotland is included; in others it is excluded. See the full set of SCHMI research papers for
more details.

is powerful, and it creates a tide of diversity – a tide felt from Sydney to Stockholm, from Toronto to Tokyo.

For half a century, ever-more immigrants have been drawn to the prosperous parts of the planet, helped on their way by more afford-able travel and encouraged, too, by the increasing ease with which it is possible to stay in touch with people back home. Figure 1.1 shows how immigrants have already grown as a share of the rich world's population and are commonly projected to continue growing, on the basis of extrapolation from current trends. Such projections, like much of the analysis in this book, frequently rely upon demographic data drawn from the census which – being collected infrequently and pro-cessed slowly – is invariably out of date. Britain's last census was in 2001 and America's in 2000; in the near-decade since, both societies have only become still more diverse.

Of course, these trends could evolve, but they are unlikely to reverse. Closing the gates is almost certainly impossible. It would also be

Figure 1.1 The growing share of immigrants as a share of host populations in the rich world – past and projection

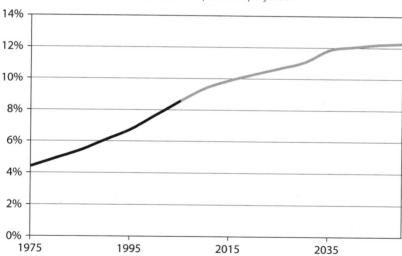

Source: OECD (2007).
Note: International immigrants as a share of host population in the 'more developed' countries. Past projections from United Nations; future projections done by OECD under assumption that today's rates of emigration and destination continue.

profoundly unwise: an ageing indigenous population needs a growing workforce to sustain it. But even if the rich world *could* close
the gates, in many nations the band of relatively young immigrants
already admitted – together with their families – would, for decades,
continue to grow as a share of the population. About the most certain prediction we can make about *any* advanced economy is that it
will be more ethnically diverse a generation down the line than it is
today.

Welcome or not, this change cannot and will not be halted any
time soon. Like the industrial and communications revolutions before
it, the diversity revolution is going to happen – in fact, it is already
under way. Its social effects may eventually compare with those of
the spinning jenny in the eighteenth century, or the internet in our
own time. This book illuminates this global phenomenon by shin-
ing a light on two very different societies: Britain, where diversity
is a comparatively recent development, and the United States, where
heterogeneity is becoming more marked, but where – for good and
for ill – it has always been seared into the national DNA.

Questions from picture-book history

Even the sketchiest awareness of the two nations' histories invites
intriguing questions about the different ways that our twin themes
of race and immigration might play out on the two sides of the Atlantic.

Every reflective American is aware that theirs is a country of
immigrants. Inside that great national icon, the Statue of Liberty, the
inscription reads: 'Give me your tired, your poor, Your huddled masses
yearning to breathe free'. That promise to welcome newcomers surely
informs Obama's claim to a uniquely American story. The pledge
has not always been honoured, as we will see, but it nonetheless
makes for a telling contrast with the fusty myths of the old-style British
nationalism, about an island people who have fended off foreigners
since 1066. On the basis of picture-book history alone, one might
wonder whether America would be the easier place to settle.

Even if the sunny ideas about immigration prove tenable, however,
the long shadow of slavery dominates the picture on race. Abolition
in the 1860s was not the end but the start of a process, a process

that weaved its way through the Jim Crow laws and the civil rights era and continues to this day. Ethnic diversity has been a feature of American life from the very beginning, though not in a happy way. The pall of slavery makes it natural to ask whether the race divide is especially marked in the US, and whether American society will struggle with managing the growing trend towards non-white immigration. And yet the old picture-book histories are rapidly being re-written to reflect the inauguration of an African American as President of the United States, so it is now equally tempting to speculate on whether the race divide is starting to heal.

Britons, too, were thoroughly embroiled in trading slaves, but slaves did not sweat on the UK's shores in the same way, so there is not the same social legacy. But it is as well to recall the British Empire's colonialism, conceived as 'the white man's burden'. That ensured that by the time the steamship *Empire Windrush* delivered the first modern black immigrants in 1948, Britain, too, was endowed with some decidedly warped ideas about race. Whether a former imperial power can treat former subjects as equal citizens is yet another compelling question.

The rest of the book

All these gripping questions jump out of a child's first book of history, but answering them involves much more than picture-book analysis. We start in the next chapter with an overview of diversity in Britain and the US (Chapter 2), setting out the number and the nature of the minorities in both, while also comparing the distinctive manner in which race and immigration is thought about in each country. After that, we dig deep into the data to try and establish three things:

- How do migrants and minorities live and work?
- How does diversity affect community life?
- How, if at all, might political debate and media coverage shape this effect on communities?

With access to millions of census records – and computers powerful enough to crunch them – we paint a newly definitive picture of living and working conditions. The main focus of Chapter 3 is on where minorities live – separated into ghettos, or integrated into the community? The chapter also reports on earlier studies covering everything from the health of migrants and minorities to their chances of ending up in jail, arguing that all sorts of social problems are more common in communities that feel compelled to live a life set apart. The extent of segregation – which varies both between our countries and between different minority communities – thus matters not just for gauging social cohesion, but also for monitoring social justice. Chapter 4 contributes to the latter, both by asking how open the world of work in Britain and America is to minorities, and by asking, in particular, just how frequently minority individuals really can clamber up the ladder of opportunity towards a better career.

The second and third questions (Chapter 5 and Chapter 6) both carry profound implications for diversity – will it, as some suggest, tend to reduce social solidarity? And if it does, can this effect be ameliorated by political will? The obvious relevance of these questions explains why they are so often already debated. The difficulty in answering them, though, has always been that there have never been enough data to cut through the chicken-and-egg confusion about exactly what causes what. Do the problems of diverse neighbourhoods reflect the fact they are mixed or instead the poverty that a racist society imposes upon them? Does intolerant talk among the elite whip up racism among the public, or does it merely reflect underlying resentment? Without a clear means to answer such questions scientifically, political prejudices tend to fill the gap – pessimists assume innate human prejudice is important, whereas optimists presume people start off as a prejudice-free blank sheet. But on both sides of the Atlantic SCHMI researchers have secured privileged access to opinion surveys, so we know the locality in which respondents live. This allows us to forge a link between individual attitudes and neighbourhood characteristics, and thereby start to displace political heat with analytical light.

Before concluding, we turn to consider the matter that has attracted so much interest in the wake of Obama's elevation – the changing place of minorities in elective politics (Chapter 7). In particular, we seek out the roots of the President's victory in majority public opinion. We ask whether – through all the ebbs and flows – underlying attitudinal currents can be discerned over the decades. This not only help us understand more clearly the arrival of a black President, but also allows us to reflect on whether the UK has seen the sort of parallel changes that would be required for a British Obama to move into No. 10.

With this final question – as with all the questions – we look at the two countries together, in part because we wish to discover differences between them. But there is also great value in establishing similarities, too, as patterns that hold in more than one country at once are relatively less likely to reflect the chance circumstances, and relatively more likely to reveal deeper social realities.

2

Two concepts in two countries: race and migration

There can be no fifty-fifty Americanism in this country. There is room here for only 100 per cent Americanism, only for those who are Americans and nothing else. (Theodore Roosevelt, speaking in 1918)[3]

We become not a melting pot but a beautiful mosaic. Different people, different beliefs, different yearnings, different hopes, different dreams. (Jimmy Carter, speaking in 1976)[4]

Diversity gives rise to some diverse reactions, as the above remarks from the 26th and 39th American presidents reveal. Is it a stepping stone towards a unified country, a destination that requires migrants and minorities to assimilate into the mainstream? Or is the multi-cultural mosaic, in Jimmy Carter's phrase, something that should be celebrated in its own right? Such questions are hotly debated in Britain, too – as indeed they are in most societies as they grapple with becoming less uniform. The research this book pulls together can inform such discussions. But to make sense of it we need first to pause and consider exactly what is meant by diversity – and its twin conceptual components, racial difference and migranthood, both of which happen to be embodied in Barack Obama.

Beyond comparison

Racial divides relate back to differences in physical inheritance, and yet the significant divides are not forever fixed; they are a product of society, and – as we shall see – they can and do change over time.

---

[3] Address to the unofficial Republican state convention in Saratoga, New York, July 1918.
[4] Speech at Pittsburgh, Pennsylvania, October 1976.

That is part of the reason terms such as 'black' and 'white' have contested meanings, while other categories such as 'Asian' signify different things in Britain and the US. There are also fierce debates among activists and academics about whether the salient ethnic divide is between black people and the rest on the one hand, or, on the other, between white people and everybody else. At first blush, our second concept – immigration – looks as if it *should* be less slippery: immigrants are people who move to a new country. As with any social schema, though, fuzziness creeps in round the edges. Do we treat the native-born children or even grandchildren of newcomers as part of an 'immigrant community'?

Most right-thinking people, like the authors of this book, would want to avoid getting lost in this sort of thick conceptual fog. But we must at least skirt round its edges to obtain a clear view of the facts in two countries at once. For data do not come ready-made; rather, they depend on what particular governments decide is important enough to count. There can even be cross-national differences in what it *makes sense* to count. Different historical experience in Britain and the US means information on race and immigration is not just labelled differently, but is actually carved up in different ways. The risk, then, is not so much that *they say tomayto and we say tomahto*, but rather that we end up talking about totally different things – at which point, it really is time to call the whole thing off. Forming a view on even the simplest question – the relative degree of diversity in our two countries – turns out to require going beyond a crude comparison of ready-made statistics.

Consider, for instance, Figure 2.1. It charts the growth of Britain's minority communities from the census, which sounds straightforward enough, but on close inspection it turns out that all sorts of judgement calls are involved. The way minorities are identified in the data changes between earlier and later years, to reflect the addition of an 'ethnicity' question to the census in 1991, something we will consider further later in the chapter. Then there are questions about the treatment of 'white minorities', ignored in this chart, as they were traditionally ignored in debates about diversity, although this is something that has recently started to change. One affected group is Irish immigrants, excluded in the chart as they are ethnically

Figure 2.1 The growing population of Britain's minorities, 1951–2001

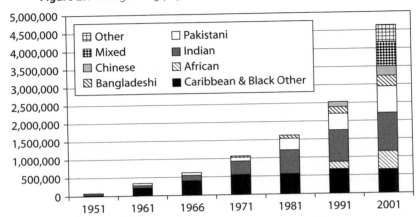

Source: Calculated from Great Britain Censuses of Population 1951–2001.
Note: 1951–81 data are largely based on place of birth; 1991 and 2001 data are based on the ethnicity question.

similar and come from a part of the British Isles, but this is a debatable decision which further underlines the way that preconceptions come into play whenever we carve society up into numbers. Indeed, if a longer historical view is taken, it becomes apparent that 'native Britishness' is itself the product of diversity. Over the millennia, the supposed pure-bred Brit was in fact distilled from a mix of the Beaker People, Celts, Romans, Angles, Saxons, Jutes, assorted Vikings, Normans, Jews, Huguenots, Russians, Dutch, Portuguese and French – all well before arrivals from the New Commonwealth began to land on British shores in the second half of the twentieth century (Winder, 2004).

Because all of this mixing happened over thousands of years, however – as opposed to in a mere two or three centuries in the American case – it has been possible to sustain the illusion of British racial homogeneity. The chart thus shows us something important, namely, the growth in that part of the British population that is *perceived to be* minority ethnic or immigrant.[5] Such communities grew

---

[5]It is telling that until very recently these two designations – 'minority ethnic' and 'immigrant' – have been treated as almost interchangeable in the UK.

from being vanishingly small immediately after the Second World War,[6] to numbering more than 4.5 million people, or around 7.5 per cent of the population, by the early years of this century. Using a more inclusive definition of minority, which includes, for example, white Irish immigrants, would give a higher figure for the census year of 2001, of 10 per cent or more. That remains the last available census but it is, of course, now somewhat out of date. In the years since, the eastward expansion of the European Union has ushered in a significant new wave of immigration. In particular, hundreds of thousands of Poles took advantage of their new right to work in the UK after their country's accession in 2004. As a result, if it were possible to draw a more up-to-date version of Figure 2.1, we can be confident that it would show even stronger growth in Britain's minority population.

The chart also reveals that the source of post-war immigration has evolved over the decades. The original influx of diversity came from India and the Caribbean, but in more recent decades the growth has originated from other places, such as Bangladesh and Africa. What these disparate parts of the planet have in common is that they once lived under the flag of the British Empire. Even though European expansion and other developments have now started to modify this pattern, it remains true that the great bulk of Britain's minority populations do retain a colonial connection.

So, Figure 2.1 tells us a lot about diversity in Britain. But now imagine trying to draw the same chart for the United States: it simply would not make any sense. The relative novelty of modern mass immigration into the UK ensures that minority and immigrant communities are effectively regarded as one and the same, and that they can be clearly identified and counted. In America, by contrast, there is no clarity about which segments of the population to treat as 'immigrant'. Classifications would change over time: immigrant communities of the 1920s and 1930s, such as the Poles of Chicago, are not considered immigrant communities today. And when they

---

[6] 'Vanishingly small', rather than non-existent, because there was a tiny black population in Great Britain for centuries before the Second World War. See Small (1994).

arrived there were already others – the Irish of New York, for example – who had ceased to be considered as newcomers. Go back far enough and every family, barring Native Americans, can be traced back to immigrants.

We could, of course, chart the overall growth of the population since the Founding Fathers – but that would tell us precious little about diversity in America. As an alternative, we could pick an arbitrary date – say, the end of the Second World War or the passage of the 1965 Immigration and Nationality Act – and concentrate on immigration after that date. But when African Americans, to say nothing of Native Americans, have been on the continent's shores for centuries, and yet retain minority status, that would not convey anything much about overall diversity either. Then there is the further question of how Hispanics – not a race as such, but a major ethnicity – would fit into the picture.

What we can do, however, is break down today's US population by ethnicity and then – separately – between natives and the foreign-born. Figures 2.2a and 2.2b do that, using the latest available official estimates. Figure 2.2a reveals that America is a far more diverse society than Britain, whereas Figure 2.1 suggested that fewer than one in ten of the 2001 population were regarded as belonging to a minority. In America in 2007, by contrast, Figure 2.2a shows that only 66 per cent of people are non-Hispanic white, so fully 34 per cent belong to one minority or another. Most of these, it is true, fall into just two camps – the blacks and the Hispanics – although the latter itself is a very diverse category. There is also a significant Asian population which compares to Britain's in proportional size, but which is very different in character. 'Asians' in Britain are overwhelmingly from the Indian subcontinent, whereas American Asians come from a great range of countries, mostly in East Asia.

The proportion of American residents born abroad is also high, as Figure 2.2b shows, running at 13 per cent or 38 million people. That is approaching *double* the relative size of Britain's total minority population in 2001 shown in Figure 2.1, even though the latter included not only actual immigrants but also their children and grandchildren. The proportion of US residents born overseas is also roughly

Figure 2.2a Ethnic diversity in America

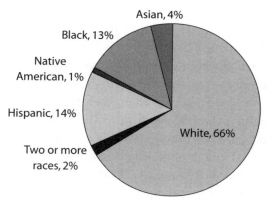

Figure 2.2b Natives and immigrants in America

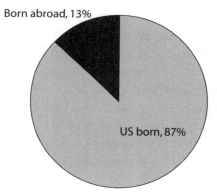

Sources: Figure 2.2a is from the US Census Bureau, 2007 estimates, accessed December 2008.[a] Figure 2.2b is from the US Census Bureau analysis of American Community Survey, accessed December 2008.[b]

Notes: In Figure 2.2a 'Hispanic' is white Hispanic only; roughly 3.5 million other Hispanics have been allocated by their given race instead. 'Native American' also includes native Alaskans, as well as Pacific islanders because this category includes native Hawaiians. In Figure 2.2b 'Born abroad' excludes American citizens born to American parents abroad.

[a]Link: www.factfinder.census.gov
[b]Link: www.factfinder.census.gov

double the total proportion of current UK residents recently estimated to have been born outside the British Isles.[7]

So, even by looking at different data in the two countries, we can conclude that the US is by far the more diverse. It is not that Britain is particularly homogeneous, but rather that America – which was always diverse – remains the world's biggest draw for migrants. As rates of worldwide immigration speeded up at the end of the twentieth century, the UK was fifth in the league table of destinations, absorbing 475,000 immigrants (net of emigrants) over the years 1995–2000. That put it somewhat behind second-place Germany (924,000), third-ranked Canada (720,000) and the Italians (588,000) who came in fourth, but just ahead of Australia (474,000), which was another important destination.[8] It was the United States, however, that led the world – and how.

America let in a net total of 6.25 million people over the period, an order of magnitude more than were admitted to Britain in absolute terms, and – even allowing for the greater population of the US – that figure implies an immigration rate which is more than twice as rapid as that in the UK. The extent of American diversity is underlined by both regional analysis and future projections. Eight of the 50 largest American metro areas already have a majority of residents from minority groups, and two more are expected to be majority-minority by the 2010 census. Indeed, non-Hispanic whites are commonly projected to become a numerical minority in the United States some time during this century (Edmonston and Passel, 1992; Massey, 1995).

What's counted and what counts

We have already seen how history affects which facts are meaningful within our two countries. National conceptions and preconceptions also determine what data are available, and which groups are regarded as 'minorities'. Transatlantic comparisons of facts and figures should

---

[7]One analysis for the Institute for Public Policy Research (IPPR) think tank put that figure at 7.5 per cent (Kyambi, 2005).

[8]All figures in this paragraph are from Ueda (2007).

thus be coloured by an appreciation of how conceptions of diversity differ. But this process works both ways: differences in the available information can shine a bright light on the contrasting ways in which race and immigration are conceived. There is no better starting point for developing a sense of how diversity is thought about in Britain and America than examining what aspects of it their governments keep tabs on. After all, societies only take the trouble to count those things that are deemed to count. And the available information tends to reflect, and reinforce, the preoccupation of academics and commentators who shape opinions and attitudes across the wider public.

The census is perhaps *the* prime source of official information, and it also serves as the template for the construction of all sorts of other facts and figures. The American census asks four relevant questions – about *birthplace*, about whether or not individuals are *Hispanic*, about *ancestry*, and about *race*. Britain also has a *birthplace* question, but its other relevant questions are different, covering *ethnicity* and *religion*. With no significant Latino population in the UK, it is hardly surprising that there is no equivalent British question on Hispanics. More striking, though, is the absence of the direct equivalent of the US *ancestry* question – an open-ended question that allows Americans to state from where they are descended. The British ethnicity question pays some regard to ancestry, although only really for minorities[9] and it is better regarded as an equivalent of the American category for race. The United States, by contrast, keeps tabs not just on its 1.2 million Arabs and 1.9 million West Indians, but also its 43 million (overwhelmingly white) residents descended from Germans and the near 2 million who trace their roots back to Wales.[10]

This official interest in heritage no doubt reflects that America is, quite consciously, a nation of immigrants. It goes hand in hand with

---

[9]The first time it was asked in 1991 it separated out black Africans and black Caribbeans, as well as differentiating racially similar Asians from India, Pakistan and Bangladesh. All whites, however, were lumped together. In 2001, boxes for white Irish and white other were introduced, but the latter was not differentiated, relying on the individual to volunteer more specific information.

[10]Figures are from the 2000 census. Available at: www.censtats.census.gov/data/US/01000.pdf

a strong tradition of sociological interest in the process of migration and how the fortunes of particular waves of immigrants fare across different generations. In Britain, by contrast, there is little official or academic interest in ethnic heritage except in so far as it gives rise to a recognisable minority ethnic identity. It is effectively assumed – rather sloppily – that everyone else is a native. The distinction between first- and second-generation immigrants is rarely deployed in British sociological analysis, a shortcoming we will address in Chapter 4.

Immigration, then, receives greater attention in America, and – unlike in Britain – it is counted separately from race and regarded as a separate concept. In part, that may reflect the early days when American immigration was something that emanated from Europe. But it is also because of the very different ways in which the idea of race has evolved on the two sides of the Atlantic. Race is now included in both censuses, albeit labelled as ethnicity in the British case. But the concept has much deeper roots in the USA. Race was included in the very first United States census in 1790, for the purposes of separately recording whites from black slaves. Slavery and its legacy made it inevitable that race would become a defining divide – in W. E. B. Du Bois's phrase a 'color line' – cleaving through American society (Du Bois, 1990 [1903]). As the white population moved westward, its conquest of American Indians and Hispanics in the Southwest exposed the new nation to what we would now call diversity, but the effect then was only to reinforce the sense of racial hierarchy. When Asians started arriving in the late nineteenth century they were racially classified by the federal government and their racial exclusion was ultimately enshrined in American immigration law until the 1950s.

The system of race classification thus developed to discriminate and exclude. Ironically, however, it was the civil rights movement that successfully pushed for it to be enshrined in the federal statistical system in order to detect, prevent and prosecute discrimination. Today, advocacy groups for racial minorities are among the staunchest defenders of racial classification, while the likes of Newt Gingrich, the conservative former speaker of the House of Representatives, talk up the idea of a colour-blind society to express discomfort with affirmative action.

In British society, by contrast, race became salient only after non-white immigration from the Commonwealth – especially India and the Caribbean – picked up during the 1950s. According to the ideals of British imperialism, a citizen of anywhere in the Empire (and later the Commonwealth) was a citizen of everywhere in the Empire. Once affordable travel started to convert this theoretical right into a practical option, however, this ideal soon gave way. By the 1960s political pressure had built for tighter controls. Britain, however, faced an oddity – those controls would not be applied against aliens, but former co-nationals, and so citizenship could not easily be used to keep foreigners out. The need for an alternative criterion for immigration was answered by effective reliance on race (Joppke, 1999). A series of laws were specifically designed with a view to cutting off 'coloured' immigration, cementing the importance of race in official British thinking. In parallel, however, British minorities and progressives – consciously inspired by the American civil rights movement – successfully pushed for race relations legislation in the 1960s and 1970s. It was in line with the increasing minority population, and increasing concern to audit social differences between the races, that an 'ethnicity' question was added to the census in 1991.

The detail of the questions on both sides of the Atlantic tells us something about where the 'color line' is drawn in each country. In the US, if there is an official binary divide, it is between black people and all others. The census has all sorts of subcategories for Asians and other minorities, but 'black or African American' is an undifferentiated block. Mixed race individuals – who until 2000 could not register as such – have historically tended to classify themselves as black. Some black minorities can, theoretically, be picked out using the ancestry question – for example, black Caribbeans. But this is rarely done in either official statistics or academic analysis. Being black, or not, is what is thought to matter. The influence of black advocacy groups – concerned to maximise the size and cohesiveness of the community they represent – is one part of the explanation. Another is racist traditions, such as the 'one drop' rule, which deemed a man a 'negro' if he had one drop of African blood. While there is no doubt that Latinos and Asians have also faced systematic discrimination in the past, contemporary scholarship tends to suggest that the race divide which now matters for life chances is indeed that which separates black people from the rest[11] – a suggestion Chapters 3 and 4 will consider in some detail.

In Britain the salient conceptual divide is between whites and others. That is reflected in the widespread official use of the phrase 'black and minority ethnic', an umbrella term for all non-whites. It is reflected, too, in an ethnicity census question which splits up non-whites into all sorts of categories – such as Black African and Bangladeshi Asian – but treats whites, more or less, as an undifferentiated block.[12] And whereas in America's 2000 census the only way to register as biracial was to pick multiple racial boxes, in the British survey of 2001 more attention was given to biraciality, with specific boxes for all sorts of mixed race categories, something which further encourages differentiation of non-whites. As we will see in the following two chapters, the life chances of many minorities are stunted in Britain. But minorities such as Bangladeshis, who would not ordinarily be classified as black, often fare worse than black communities.

We now turn to the one important thing that is officially counted in Britain but not America. In 2001, a voluntary question on religion was added to the British census. While England retains an established church, the legal separation of church and the American state goes back at least to the Bill of Rights in 1791. The American authorities are deeply reluctant to collect data on religion – indeed, if answers such as 'Jewish' or 'Muslim' are written in on the ancestry question, these are disregarded.

But the transatlantic difference is not just a question of what statistics are collected. The relationship between minority faiths – Islam in particular – and wider society is seen as being at the heart of community relations in Britain. The connection was reinforced by the home-grown terrorism of British Muslims which hit London in July 2005. One of the many occasions on which it has fuelled heated arguments about multiculturalism arose when, in 2006, British

[11]See, for example, Kasinitz (2004) or Bean and Stevens (2003).
[12]'White Irish' was introduced in 2001 and was ticked by a little more than 1 per cent; a slightly larger proportion, 2.7 per cent, classified themselves as 'White Other', but this covers everything from Eastern Europeans to Australians.

Cabinet minister Jack Straw branded the full face veil, worn by a minority of Muslim women, a 'visible statement of separation and of difference'.[13] But religion in general and Islam in particular are rarely referenced at all in American debates about immigration – faith is simply not seen as separating minorities from the majority in the same way.

It is not, of course, that America lacks religious diversity – or even a significant number of Muslims. The Pew Center for the Study of Religion estimates that there are about 2.35 million Muslims in the US, which is more, in absolute terms, than the total 1.5 million counted in Britain's 2001 census. Of America's adult Muslims, two-thirds were born overseas, something that might be expected to make them stand out more. But one thing that no doubt helps prevent religion from becoming a dividing line is that America's Muslims do better in socio-economic terms – the Pew Center dubbed them 'middle class and mostly mainstream',[14] a fair reflection on how they perform in terms of income and qualification. That makes for quite a contrast with Britain, where Pakistanis and Bangladeshis tend to be at the bottom of the heap, as the next two chapters will show. There is, however, another difference, not just with Britain, but with Western Europe as a whole. Secular Europe sees religion as a barrier to inclusion and Islam as irreconcilable to the West, whereas in the US it is generally seen as a bridge – something that can help turn immigrants into Americans, and help give them a sense of belonging to the United States. For example, in both the wave of immigration at the end of the nineteenth century from southern and eastern Europe and the current wave from Latin America and Asia, shared adherence to the Catholic Church was an important bond between many immigrants and many native-born Americans, so the American Catholic Church has played an important role in integrating the immigrants into American society. That US–European distinction in attitudes towards the role of religion in immigration not only holds in

---

[13]The remark was written in a column in a local newspaper, the *Lancashire Evening Telegraph*, which is reproduced in full by the BBC at: www.news.bbc.co.uk/1/hi/uk_politics/5413470.stm
[14]See: www.pewresearch.org/pubs/483/muslim-americans

popular discourse, but also shapes the terms of social scientific inquiry (Foner and Alba, 2008).

Same difference

We have seen that one historical transatlantic contrast in the conception of diversity – a contrast reflected in the censuses – is that in Britain race and immigration are regarded as inextricably linked, whereas in America they have been regarded as distinct issues. This reflects national experience. America was used to racial difference from the very beginning, albeit initially in the twisted form of slavery. It also has long experience in receiving immigration. But there was traditionally no overlap between the two concepts of racial diversity and immigration. Throughout the nineteenth and early twentieth centuries, while generations of established African Americans continued to toil, successive waves of immigration brought more and more white Europeans. Britain, however, was used to neither racial difference nor immigration until the post-war era when diversity suddenly arrived in a single package, in the form of non-white immigration from the Commonwealth.

Today, however, the pattern has changed on both sides of the Atlantic. Indeed, it has been changing so rapidly that there are appreciable changes over the near-decade since the last censuses were carried out, in 2000 in the USA and in 2001 in the UK. Figures 2.3a and 2.3b draw on more recent sources to reveal the share of the current flow of immigrants provided by each of the top ten countries for both Britain and America. Easily the biggest single chunk in Britain (33 per cent) are now white workers (and dependants) coming from Poland. These figures pre-date the credit crunch which – by making work harder to come by in the UK – has dissuaded some Eastern Europeans from coming to Britain, and persuaded others who were already here to leave. Even if the influx has slowed for the moment, however, white immigration from the East is likely to continue to be important over the longer term.

In the US, meanwhile, modern immigrants are overwhelmingly either non-white or Hispanic. Mexicans represent the biggest single slice on the chart – a slice that would be bigger still if illegal

Figure 2.3a The relative importance of the top ten sources of immigrants flowing into Britain, 2006–7

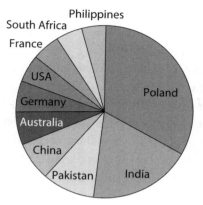

Figure 2.3b The relative importance of the top ten sources of immigrants flowing into America, 2006

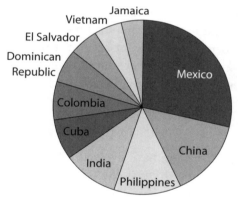

Sources: Figure 2.3a, 2007 Total International Migration estimates supplied by the Office for National Statistics based on International Passenger Survey. Figure 2.3b from Migration Information Source calculations for 2006, available at: www.migrationinformation.org/datahub/countrydata/data.cfm, and based on the US Department of Homeland Security Yearbook of Immigration Statistics.

Notes: Figure 2.3a estimates include only those who intend to stay in the UK for 12 months or more. International Passenger Survey (IPS) is adjusted for asylum seekers and their dependants, flows from the Irish Republic and the switcher adjustments for those whose intentions change. The American data records persons admitted for legal permanent residence during the 12-month fiscal year ending in October of the year designated. They exclude illegal immigrants who do not have the paperwork in train. The overwhelming majority of these are Mexicans and other Hispanics. Given that these are similar in number to permanent legal immigrants (Passel and Suro, 2006), their inclusion would greatly increase the share of Mexico and some of the other Latin American countries.

immigrants were factored in – and they are very much seen as being a minority, owing to their Hispanic status.[15] And indeed, immigrants from *all* of the top ten places would qualify either as Hispanic minorities, or – as in the case of the Chinese and the Indians – racial ones.

So, America is now experiencing non-white immigration and Britain is experiencing the white variety. The intriguing question for the future is whether this will produce a convergence of concepts about diversity – a sameness in thinking about difference. Britain's experience of mass white immigration is new, having been triggered by the eastward expansion of the EU in 2004, and that is probably too recent to turn around the supertanker of academic and official thinking. But non-white migration into America has been becoming increasingly prevalent ever since the immigration laws were liberalised in 1965. It has already had a marked effect on the way academics think about race and immigration. In the 1980s the distinctions between race relations research and immigration research began to break down in the universities, as scholars began to study the post-1965 wave of immigrants. If, to misquote Keynes, political men are unwitting slaves to some defunct sociologist, it might be only a matter of time before race relations and immigration come to be linked in the American public debate as they have always been linked in Britain.

Melting pots and salad bowls

The concept of race may have evolved differently in Britain and America, but one thing the two countries have in common is that race is considered important. That puts them at odds with the official stance in other western European countries, such as France, which explicitly forbids the collection of racial data, and Germany, where diversity is debated in terms of birthplace and citizenship, rather than skin colour. The shared belief that race, an idea that relates to physical difference, is an important dimension of diversity makes it seem less plausible in the UK or the US that all difference can be

---

[15]Passel (2005) finds that the majority (57 per cent) of illegals are Mexicans, and that another 24 per cent are from the rest of South America, so that all told 80 per cent of illegal immigrants are from Latin America.

melted away through energetic assimilation. If difference is here to stay, that famous American icon, the melting pot, may be a less fitting image for society than a salad bowl – in which different elements are mixed up together, but each element remains recognisably distinct.

In terms of the presidential views set out at the beginning of this chapter, the attention paid to racial difference in the US has tended to favour the likes of Jimmy Carter over Teddy Roosevelt. The salad bowl and the melting pot have both had their advocates in Britain too. The former Home Secretary, Roy Jenkins, gave a celebrated expression of the salad bowl view when he explained in 1966 that integration should be not about 'a flattening process of assimilation' but instead about the promotion of 'equal opportunity accompanied by cultural diversity in an atmosphere of mutual tolerance'. The former Conservative Cabinet minister Norman Tebbit was widely suspected of racism when, in 1990, he suggested that an important marker of minorities being regarded as British was whether they would support the English cricket team against their ancestral teams, those of Pakistan or the West Indies, for example. Indeed, it was unclear how white Australian residents, or for that matter, England-baiting Scottish sports fans, would be treated by the 'cricket test'. But – on the most generous reading – Tebbit was propounding a melting pot strategy, arguing that newcomers could be tolerated so long as they surrendered their differences. Tebbit, however, was already out of government when he made his remarks, and in Britain the prevalent official approach has long been to promote tolerance for diversity, rather than attempting to engineer sameness.

Recent concern about Islamism has encouraged a degree of reappraisal in the UK, seen, for example, in the creation in 2006 of a Commission on Integration and Cohesion to examine the 'tensions' that diversity can cause. But even Ruth Kelly, the Cabinet minister who set up that body, said at much the same time that 'it is the very diversity of Britain which underpins our success, our dynamism and our international reputation'.[16] In the same year, the government was so determined to push through controversial legislation to protect the sensitivities of religious minorities that it ran into a rare defeat on the

[16]See: www.communities.gov.uk/archived/speeches/corporate/values-responsibilities

floor of the House of Commons, when MPs concerned about free speech forced through an amendment. The British authorities, then, continue to think more in terms of the salad bowl than the melting pot.

The same is true in contemporary America, although a transatlantic difference in terminology prevents some Britons from grasping that. In particular, when American academics talk about the 'assimilation' of immigrants into their society they refer to a process that 'occurs spontaneously and often unintended in the course of interaction between majority and minority groups' (Alba and Nee, 1997). It is also a process that must be understood as a two-way street, with the American mainstream changing to accommodate newcomers just as surely as the newcomers may change as they fit into their new society (Alba and Nee, 2003). By contrast, in Britain, as in the rest of Europe, 'assimilation' is not seen as something spontaneous, but rather as a top-down process imposed on newcomers which requires them to conform to the habits of the majority. This interpretation owes something to the French tradition of granting citizenship to non-Europeans – initially in the colonies, and later to immigrants within France itself – conditional on their adopting French culture and customs. But as we have seen – for a mix of good and ill reasons from discriminatory immigration control to civil rights campaigns – race gained a salience in Britain and America which helped ensure that in neither country is citizenship seen as something that makes all differences disappear.

Liberal Britons who bristle against American talk of assimilation, then, frequently misunderstand what it means. The spontaneous mixing and familiarisation of different communities does, of course, happen in Britain too, but goes instead by the name of 'integration'. While this chapter has sought to highlight differences in the British and American experience and conception of diversity, one important similarity is that – for the most part – cultural difference is not seen as something that can be washed away in either country. There is, however, a major attitudinal difference when it comes to geographic divisions between racial communities in the form of residential segregation. This is something American commentators have spent a great deal of time worrying about, whereas the British have tended to be much more relaxed. The next chapter aims to find out why that might be.

3

Home truths: how minorities live

Had Elvis been English, he would probably never have recorded *In the Ghetto*. As it was, he was American, and even in his day concerns about minorities living a life set geographically apart were widespread in the United States. The melting pot myth holds that while newly arrived minorities may find themselves in the rough part of town, they and their children will gradually move into more prosperous places. This myth has a powerful hold, and when it fails to play out, Americans discern a problem.

Ghettos are no more regarded as something that racial minorities – and in particular African Americans – have chosen than are the 'separate but equal' schools which the Supreme Court ruled illegal in *Brown v. Board of Education*. Since that 1954 ruling, the great arguments over civil rights have frequently turned on residential segregation – from the Fair Housing Act, rushed through in the aftermath of Martin Luther King Jr's assassination in 1968, to the legal wrangling over school bussing through the 1970s, the 1980s and beyond. When Hurricane Katrina burst the levees of New Orleans in 2005, the suffering of the city's majority-black districts – and the initial neglect of this suffering by the authorities – showed how the ghetto still blighted the state of the twenty-first century Union.

Attitudes could hardly be more different in Britain. The question of where people live has traditionally been treated as peripheral to race relations. After the July 2005 terrorist attacks on London, the chair of the (now defunct) Commission for Racial Equality, Trevor Phillips, sought to challenge the orthodoxy with a speech that put residential segregation centre-stage (Phillips, 2005). He claimed 'some districts are on their way to becoming fully fledged ghettoes – black holes into which no-one goes without fear and trepidation, and from which no-one ever escapes undamaged'. He warned of 'marooned communities', 'evolving their own lifestyles, playing by their own rules' which would leave Britons 'eyeing each other uneasily over the fences of our differences'. The 'American nightmare' in prospect, he said, was of 'crime, no-go areas and chronic cultural conflict'. The speech met with a violent reaction. Phillips's predecessor at the Commission, Lord Herman Ouseley, branded it 'totally wrong',[17] and a few months later London mayor Ken Livingstone accused Phillips of 'pandering to the right'.[18] Some of this no doubt reflected Phillips's integrationist views on everything from religious dress in schools to minority languages, and some his highly selective use of the evidence. But part of the controversy arose because in Britain, unlike America, the working assumption is that minorities choose where they live, and claiming that society would benefit from minorities being less concentrated is thus seen as tantamount to telling them what to do.

One unexpected consequence of this transatlantic contrast is that the ideological polarity of debates about segregation in the two countries is reversed. In the US progressives (or 'liberals') seem especially concerned about ethnic segregation (having in mind the imposed segregation of the Jim Crow era), whereas conservatives are much more relaxed about allowing people to live where they want and associate with whomever they wish, even if that leads to de facto segregation and lily-white social clubs. In Britain, by contrast, it is those on the Left who are most relaxed about ethnic segregation, and those on the Right who are most likely to denounce ethnic enclaves as contrary to national unity.

In this chapter we will explore whether these transatlantic sensibilities reflect a difference in facts on the ground. We first compare the residential concentration of African Americans in particular, to that of British minorities in general. Next we explore how levels of segregation have evolved over time – looking for any signs of the increased UK segregation that Trevor Phillips described. We

---

[17]See: www.news.bbc.co.uk/1/hi/uk/4273414.stm
[18]See: www.dailymail.co.uk/news/article-424179/ken-livingstone-brands-race-boss-dud.html

establish that the entrenched nature of African American segregation is distinctive, when compared both with segregation in Britain and with that affecting other minorities in the United States. We then reflect on the hand history may have played in shaping the ghetto and turn to consider its impact on other aspects of life, most importantly education.

All together now?

In the last chapter we learned that America was a much more diverse country than Britain, with fully one-third of its residents coming from outside the majority non-Hispanic white group, compared with – depending on exactly who is included – something around one in ten Britons who qualify as minorities. But how far Britons and Americans experience diversity also depends on how far different ethnic groups mix. If minorities live entirely parallel lives then neither the salad bowl nor the melting pot is the appropriate metaphor, for there will be little coming together of communities at all.

The differing size of British and American minorities complicates the comparison. Members of American minorities will, all else being equal, be much more likely to live around other people from minorities because they are so much more numerous. One way to reduce the potential for confusion would be to compare the concentration of *all* British minorities with the one American minority whose segregation has traditionally been a particular concern; the 13 per cent of the population classed as black. Figures 3.1a and 3.1b make this comparison using data from each country's latest census. Figure 3.1a shows the proportion of whites and minorities in England and Wales who live in wards where minorities represent particular proportions of the population; likewise, for America, Figure 3.1b shows the proportion of white and black people who live in census tracts with given proportions of blacks.

For white people, the British and American results are strikingly similar – the overwhelming majority live in neighbourhoods that are less racially mixed than the country as a whole, evidence of a degree of segregation. Just over 80 per cent of whites in both Britain and America live in neighbourhoods where non-whites (or in the US chart,

Figure 3.1a Percentage of white and minority ethnic Britons who
live in wards with different percentages of minority ethnic residents
in England and Wales

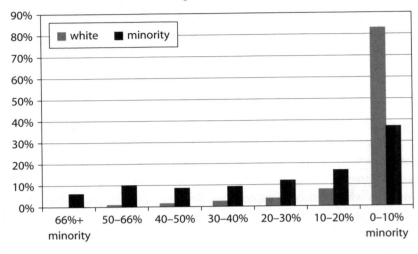

Figure 3.1b Percentage of white and black Americans who live in census tracts
with different percentages of black residents

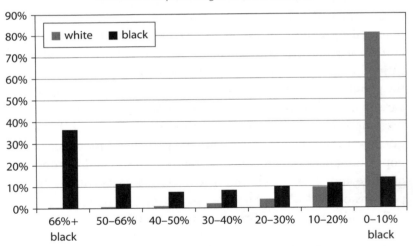

Source: Calculated by Peach (2009) from Great Britain Censuses of Population 2001 and
the United States Census, 2000.
Note: The average population of a US tract is around 4,000; the average population of
an English ward is around 8,000.

more specifically black people) represent less than 10 per cent of the
population. Digging into the data behind the charts reveals it is often
much less than 10 per cent – in the US, for instance, around a third
(35 per cent) of all whites live in tracts where less than 1 per cent of
the population are African American.

For non-whites, however, striking transatlantic differences emerge
– British minorities tend to spread out, while African Americans pile
up. Figure 3.1b shows that fully 36 per cent of African Americans
live in tracts with very few whites where blacks represent two-thirds
or more of the population, and that virtually half (48 per cent) of
the total live in black majority neighbourhoods. This tendency to cluster means that only one American black in seven (14 per cent) lives
in areas where blacks are in a small minority of less than 10 per cent
of the local population. In Britain, in sharp contrast, Figure 3.1a reveals
a clear plurality of non-whites living in places that are 90 per cent
or more white. A mere 6 per cent of British minorities live in places
where they number more than two-thirds of the population, and only
16 per cent live in wards with even a bare majority of non-whites.

Concentrate on the densest ghettos of all (not shown separately
on the charts) and the contrasts become even starker. Just 2 per cent
of English minorities live in districts where they represent over
80 per cent of the population compared to 27 per cent of American
blacks. Not a single English or Welsh ward has a minority concentration above 90 per cent, but fully 17 per cent of African Americans live
in such tracts, and indeed a handful (0.2 per cent) live in tracts where
the population is totally (100 per cent) black. In sum, British non-whites
do not seem to be at all ghettoised, at least by American standards.

The above comparison has the merit of being in line with the dis-
cussion in the previous chapter as to where the salient colour line
fell in each country – between whites and the rest in Britain, and
between blacks and the rest in the United States. And, on the face of
it, it might seem to tell us all we need to know about why ghettos
have been so much more of a concern in the US than Britain – there
is simply no British equivalent to a large number of American communities which Figure 3.1b suggests have only very few whites. In
other words, it suggests that the ghetto is a distinctively American
phenomenon.

But this simple analysis can be criticised for failing to compare like with like – the combined British ethnic minority population is somewhat smaller in relative terms than the African American community. Besides, properly speaking, a ghetto is a concentration of one particular minority, and the distinctive history of Britain's various minority ethnic groups means they are likely to be segregated to very different degrees. So far, however, we have lumped all British minorities together. To disentangle them and then compare each with the African American community, what we really need is an indicator of segregation that we can calculate for each one which will not be distorted by the fact that they have very different sizes. The Index of Dissimilarity (ID) is the right tool for the job.

The ID score gives a thermometer reading of the closeness of groups, and therefore of the potential for interaction between them. Its range is from 0 (no segregation) through to 1 (total segregation), or equivalently from 0 per cent to 100 per cent. Box 3.1 gives more details and explains how the ID is calculated. But to start making use of the index, it is enough to know that readings are commonly interpreted as follows:

- ID of 0 to 0.39: low segregation
- ID of 0.4 to 0.49: moderate segregation
- ID of 0.5 to 0.59: moderately high segregation
- ID of 0.6 to 0.69: high segregation
- ID of 0.7 to 1.0: very high segregation

As well as being unaffected by the size of the group, this index has two great advantages. First, the ID value has a straightforward interpretation that can be expressed in plain English: it is the percentage of *either* of the two groups being compared that would have to move between neighbourhoods if they were to be spread out in the same way as the other group. Secondly, ID has been deployed in sociological study for more than half a century, so we can readily compare our own calculations from the census with calculations from earlier studies in order to chart changes over time.

No single index, however, can capture every aspect of a phenomenon with as many aspects as segregation. Some of these aspects – such as the chances of avoiding contact with other groups – *do* depend on how numerous one's own group is, so indices other than the size-invariant ID come into play, but each index has its own snags. Indices can only ever be the scaffolding for the understanding, not the building itself. For simplicity, we will concentrate on ID scores, but in support of our conclusion we will cite studies that deploy a battery of different metrics.[19]

Box 3.1 Measuring segregation: calculating the Index of Dissimilarity (ID)

Imagine a totally segregated city. Some neighbourhoods would be all black, and some would be all white: there would be no overlap at all. Now imagine a city as assimilated as is possible – with a totally even ethnic spread, each tract would contain exactly the same percentage of the city's total black population and the city's total white population. We want to gauge how far reality lies between these two extremes. The Index of Dissimilarity does this by totting up half the (absolute) difference between the proportion of all blacks and the proportion of all whites found in each neighbourhood.

Imagine a square city of four tracts: A, B, C and D. Imagine whites are evenly distributed across town, with 25 per cent of the city's total in each, while blacks are unevenly distributed, with 10 per cent living in A, 20 per cent in B, 30 per cent in C and 40 per cent in D. Take the black population from the white in each case (giving, in A, B, C and D, respectively, +15, +5, −5 and −15). If we ignore the positive and negative signs, these percentage difference figures add up to a total of 40, but only half that proportion of blacks would need to move to replicate the distribution of whites (or vice versa) and so we halve our total in order to calculate an ID score of 20. Intuitively, the reason only half that number need to move is that each black person who moves from a predominantly black neighbourhood into a white neighbourhood is not only reducing black ghettoisation by one person but also diluting white segregation to the same extent.

The identical argument applies in reverse when a white person moves into a disproportionately black area. If sufficient whites move out of tracts where blacks are currently under-represented and into tracts where blacks are over-represented integration is also achieved. If 5 per cent of all whites moved from B to C and another 15 per cent of the total moved from A to D (so that 20 per cent in total had moved), then the proportion of whites in each tract would be, respectively, 10, 20, 30 and 40 – exactly the same as for blacks. Thus the ID score of 20 is the proportion of *either* the black *or* the white population that would have to move to achieve full integration.

---

[19]In particular, see Massey and Denton (1993), who explore the African American ghetto by combining five different measures of unevenness – Centralisation, Consolidation, Concentration, the 'P*' index of segregation and ID itself – to define 'hyper-segregation'. This approach confirms that the African American ghetto possesses a special intensity.

Slow-cook vs. no-cook American melting pots

As an immigrant nation, America has fostered a great tradition of studying the fortunes of newcomers which is unmatched in Britain. The Chicago School of Sociology, whose founders included Robert Park, believed that assimilation took place as successive waves of immigrants moved out of the deprived inner city – each group of newcomers displacing its predecessors, who moved further out of town, a little like waves rippling out from the centre when a rock is thrown into a pond.

Thus new immigrants settled in dense clusters in the inner city, and displaced the immigrant group that immediately preceded them. In turn, the group dislodged from the city centre moved to the edges of town, into ethnic villages perhaps, and in doing so displaced their own predecessors out and on towards the wealthier suburbs. As they moved outwards, the minorities mixed with the wider society and became more assimilated. 'The Chinatowns, the Little Sicilies, and the other so-called "ghettos"', Park asserted, are something that 'the keener, the more energetic and the more ambitious very soon emerge from . . . and move into an area of second immigrant settlement, or perhaps into a cosmopolitan area in which the members of several immigrant and racial groups live side by side' (Park, 1926).

Figure 3.2 tracks the assimilation of the Polish community into the mainstream of Chicago society between 1930 and 1990 by charting the declining ID score. As a community that arrived in the late nineteenth and early twentieth century, Poles were relative newcomers in 1930, with a comparatively high ID score of 0.51. Recall that the ID can only vary between 0 and 1, so this means they were at that time closer to being totally segregated than totally integrated. Analysis by Thomas Philpott (1978) suggests that among European minorities, Poles at this time were by some distance the most segregated. Most members of other European groups, such as the Italians and the Swedish, did not live in recognised enclaves, and even within such enclaves they did not constitute a majority. In 1930 around three in five Poles (62 per cent) did, however, live within Polish enclaves, and within these localities Poles represented a slight majority (54 per cent) of the population. This explains the comparatively high ID score for Poles.

Figure 3.2 Assimilation of Poles into Chicago society, measured by dwindling ID scores for the community, 1930–90

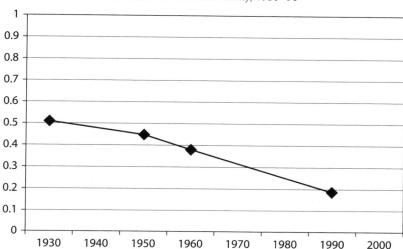

Sources: 1930 and 1950 figures from Duncan and Lieberson (1959) table 1; 1960 figure from Taeuber and Taeuber (1964) table 1; 1990 figure calculated in Peach (2009).
Notes: 1930–60 figures refer to Polish-born individuals; 1990 figures refer to individuals with Polish heritage. While all the figures shown in this chart are comparable, they should be taken as indicative rather than absolute, as they are derived from different studies in which city boundaries and ethnic dividing lines were defined in slightly different ways.

Even in 1930, however, Chicago's Poles were far from being universally ghettoised. The figures just given imply that many Poles already lived elsewhere in the city, and that even those living within the enclave had been exposed to the near-half of their neighbours who were in fact non-Poles. From this starting point, the chart shows that Poles integrated in a remarkably steady manner. The ID score dwindles from 0.51 in 1930 to 0.45 in 1950, to 0.38 in 1960 and then to a highly assimilated score of 0.19 in 1990, powerful evidence of the slow-bubbling melting pot doing its job. Further support for the proposed 'rippling waves' mechanism of suburban assimilation was uncovered when demographers started to chart how far out from the city centre successive immigrant communities lived. Ford (1950) showed that between 1890 and 1940, there was a great wave of movement from central Chicago to the suburbs for several European minorities. At the start of the period, the clear majority of Poles lived within the three-mile zone from the city centre, whereas by the end large pro-portions lived five, six or even more miles out.

The assimilation theory performed so well that academics had no inhibitions in extending it to another distinctive 'immigrant' wave of the mid-twentieth century, that of African Americans from the south to the north of the USA.

African Americans were once a rarity in the northern states. As of 1920 they made up more than 10 per cent of the population (and often substantially more) in 13 former slaving states, mainly in the south.[20] Beyond these 13 states, however, African Americans represented less – and generally much less – than 10 per cent of the population. Where white southerners had long relied on the sweat of the black man, the need for cheap labour in the north had tradi-tionally been answered by migration instead: as of 1920, in every American state of the north and the Pacific west, first-generation immigrants constituted more than 10 per cent of the population (Willcox, 1931). The First World War, however, had closed off lines of European immigration, and amid the economic instability of its aftermath, laws were passed that permanently restricted the inflow – particularly the inflow from the poorer parts of Europe. Capitalism's appetite for cheap labour, however, did not go away, and millions of African Americans – who sought opportunities unavail-able in the legally segregated South – answered it, through Great Northward Migration between 1910 and 1960.

Northern cities, such as Chicago, were among the main destina-tions, and African American 'immigrants' arrived to live in cramped inner-city areas. But the leading light of Chicago sociology, Philip Hauser, was perfectly confident that the melting pot would work its magic once more. 'The Negro migrant to the city', he wrote in a journal edited by Henry Kissinger, 'will without question, follow the same pattern of mobility blazed by the successive waves of immigrants who settled our central cities . . . In time, [he] will diffuse through the metropolitan area and occupy outlying suburban as well as central city areas' (Hauser, 1958).

---

[20]All 11 Confederacy states, as well as the two former slave states of Delaware and Maryland.

Figure 3.3 Poles assimilate but not African Americans: ID scores for the two communities in Chicago, 1930–2000

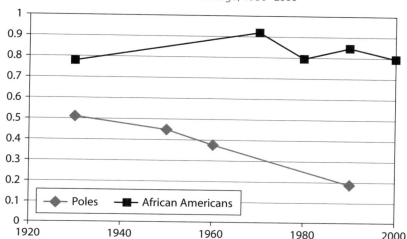

Sources: See Figure 3.2 for Polish sources. African American figures: 1930 from Taeuber and Taeuber (1964), 1970 and 1980 from Massey and Denton (1993), 1990 from Peach (2009) and 2000 from Iceland *et al.* (2002).

Notes: For the Polish series, 1930–60 figures refer to Polish-born individuals; 1990 figures refer to individuals with Polish heritage. While all the figures shown in this chart are comparable, they should be taken as indicative rather than absolute, as they are derived from different studies in which city boundaries and ethnic dividing lines were defined in slightly different ways.

Figure 3.3, however, makes plain that the Chicago School's theories failed the African American test. Once again, we plot the steady decline in the ID scores for Poles in the city; this time, however, we chart the IDs for African Americans alongside it. Two things stand out. First, African American segregation *was always much higher.* Some years the score is around 0.8, in others nearer to 0.9, but in every case African Americans are much more segregated than the Poles ever were. Secondly, whereas the segregation of Chicago's Poles diminishes with each passing census, with African Americans in the same city, *there is no trend to assimilation at all.*

Chicago, then, does not seem to be such a sweet home to African Americans, at least not if the measure is the extent to which they have been able to assimilate into the city. But is it a special case? Figure 3.4 plots trends in ID scores measured over all metropolitan areas across

Figure 3.4 Nationwide segregation of African Americans is edging down but remains higher than for other minorities: ID scores 1980–2000

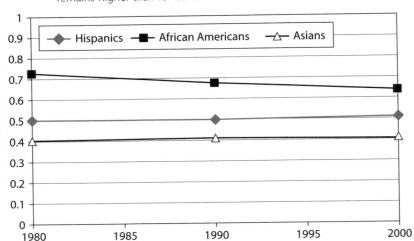

Source: Iceland *et al.* (2002).
Note: Calculated from tract-level census data across all metropolitan areas in the United States.

the United States as a whole, not only for African Americans, but also for the other big minority groups – Hispanics and Asians. The 'all-metropolitan' African American ID scores are markedly lower than the scores for Chicago – ranging from 0.73 to 0.64 over 1980–2000 – compared to the scores in Chicago over the same period, which we have seen are 0.80 more. Thus Chicago is more ghettoised than the United States as a whole. Unlike in Chicago, when America is considered as a whole there *is* an appreciable trend towards integration over recent decades, something we will seek to explain towards the end of this chapter, and a process that is likely to have continued over the ten years since America's last census was conducted.

Still, even in 2000 African Americans remain closer to total segregation than full integration. Their ID scores charted in Figure 3.4 are also far higher than those for Hispanics (who consistently score around 0.5) and even more markedly higher than those for Asians (which run at around 0.4). The inter-minority contrasts are starker than they first appear, since America's black community is as old as the nation, and even in northern cities it has now been established for several generations, whereas the population of Asians and Hispanics is largely made up of newcomers arriving since the mid-1960s. If the optimistic traditional 'rippling waves' account of assimilation was right, the rapid continuing inflow of Hispanics and Asians in recent years should be working to *increase* the relative segregation of these groups. Yet overall, both groups have ID scores which flatline, suggesting that the longer established among them are assimilating rapidly. There are, of course, black immigrants too, from Africa and the Caribbean, and in cities such as New York they are very numerous indeed. Peculiarly, however, these black immigrants are often actually *less* segregated than black people of American lineage.

All this creates the impression that America may indeed be good at assimilating immigrants, but that it retains a special problem with its native African American community. It reinforces, once again, the claim that the 'color line' which counts most in America is that between blacks and the rest.

To sum up, in the city of Chicago the slow-cooking melting pot works for most minorities, but seems to have done no cooking at all for African Americans; a finding supported by a long line of previous research.[21] More up-to-date nationwide figures suggest that this is a little too gloomy, and that African American segregation is on the decline. Nonetheless, the nationwide picture makes it plain that the melting pot works at very different speeds for different minorities – and works most slowly of all for the black community.

English enclaves and American ghettos

'Increasingly', said the Commission for Racial Equality's head Trevor Phillips in that controversial 2005 speech we quoted at the top of the chapter, 'we live with our own kind'. He went on to claim that cities

---

[21]Lieberson (1963) looked at many American cities in the late nineteenth and early twentieth centuries, and found only two cases where African Americans are less segregated than white minorities – Boston, in 1880, where ID scores were somewhat lower for blacks than for Italians, Poles and Russians, and Columbus, in 1910, where native-born whites were somewhat less segregated from African Americans than they were from foreign-born whites. Other than that, though, African Americans were always more segregated than others – and they were so without exception after the post-First World War Great Northward Migration.

such as Leicester and Bradford were 'sleepwalking into segregation' which resembled that of Miami and Chicago. The suggestion seemed to be that instead of being a melting pot, British society operated like a centrifuge, which applies force to separate milk from cream, hurling different ethnic elements apart.

Phillips made plain he was more concerned about some ethnic minorities than others, and, in particular, South Asians. But even within that broad grouping, differences in background give reason to expect that minorities will assimilate in different ways. The Indian community is mostly descended from the prosperous peasants of Gujarat and the Punjab, and there is also a well-to-do professional element, boosted by the 1970s inflow of persecuted East African Indians, largely of the mercantile class. Britain's Pakistanis, by contrast, were largely dispossessed, many of them displaced by the building of the Mangla Dam. The Bangladeshi community, the most recent to arrive, comes chiefly from the isolated Sylhet region. As well as background and class position, there is also the question of faith and culture. Pakistanis and Bangladeshis are commonly Muslims, and within both communities there is a tradition – enforced to varying degrees – of discouraging contact between unmarried women and men, an approach which might foster segregation.

We can establish the facts about what all this might mean for integration using the ethnicity question that has been asked in the last two censuses. Figure 3.5 tracks the average ID score for each minority across England's most diverse urban centres, in 1991 and 2001. The chart shows huge variation between minorities, with 2001 ID scores ranging from 0.37 for Caribbeans through to 0.61 for the most recently arrived ethnic minority, the Bangladeshis. Figure 3.4 showed that across all metropolitan areas, American Asians had an ID score of around 0.4, and Hispanics had a score of around 0.5. Both these American groups contain a high proportion of first-generation immigrants, but they are markedly less segregated than Britain's Bangladeshis and, indeed, they are no more segregated than Britain's Pakistani community (whose ID is shown as 0.51), which has been established for longer. For many immigrants, then, these figures suggest that segregation may indeed be at least as much of an issue in Britain as it is for American immigrants.

Figure 3.5 Segregation varies between British minorities but is declining for all of them: average ID scores across a range of cities, 1991–2001

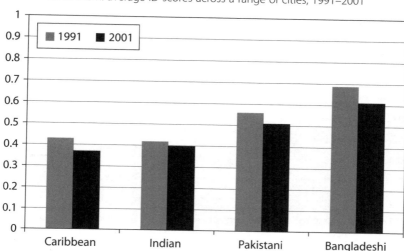

Source: Peach (2009), table 6.
Note: ID scores shown are the unweighted average of the scores across the 14 chief metropolitan centres of ethnic minority settlement in England.

However, for all of the British groups segregation is less marked than it is for African Americans, and indeed for every minority it is shown to have declined in the decade to 2001. Only Bangladeshis (0.61) have a 2001 score which even approaches the all-metropolitan areas figure for African Americans (0.65). And it bears repeating that Bangladeshis are relatively recent immigrants. The rapid decline in their segregation between 1991 and 2001 suggests that the melting pot is working more rapidly for them than it has ever done for African Americans.

Lacking an ethnicity question before 1991, the census precludes taking the same analysis any further back for England as a whole, but by exploiting previous studies we can take a longer view for the Afro-Caribbean community in London. Figure 3.6 shows that community's assimilation over time, and compares this to the residential segregation affecting African Americans in the United States's own number one city, New York. African American New Yorkers not only started out far more segregated, but have remained consistently segregated since the 1960s. In London, segregation not only was less

Figure 3.6 Afro-Caribbeans have progressively assimilated in London while African Americans in New York have continued to live apart: ID scores 1940–2000

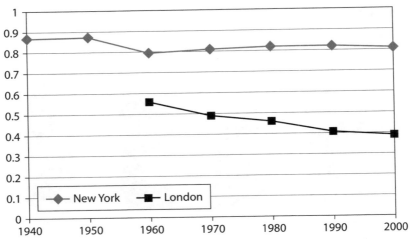

Sources: 1940–60 New York figures from Taeuber and Taeuber (1965); 1970 and 1980 New York figures from Massey and Denton (1993); 1990 New York figure from Denton (1994); 2000 New York figure from Iceland *et al.* (2002). All London figures for 1961–91 from Peach (1996); for 2001 from Peach (2009).
Notes: New York figures 1940–60 are calculated at block level, and at the level of the census tract thereafter. London figures are calculated at ward level, and relate to the census years 1961, 1971, 1981, 1991 and 2001. London Black Caribbeans identified using country of birth 1961–81, and the census ethnicity question thereafter. See Peach (1996) and Peach (2009).

pronounced to begin with, but also declined so markedly that by the census of 2001 London's Afro-Caribbeans were only *half* as segregated as African Americans in New York.

As we have seen, however, Afro-Caribbeans are the most residentially integrated of England's minorities, and – as Trevor Phillips argued – segregation is not the same issue in London as in other parts of the country. When Phillips spoke of American-style ghettos in our midst, he was thinking specifically of the enclaves of Indians and Pakistanis in cities of the Midlands and the North, such as Leicester and Bradford. If we home in on these examples do we really find anything that compares with the American ghetto?

Figures 3.7a and 3.7b make the comparison, contrasting the distribution of the black population of Chicago and Miami, respectively,

Figure 3.7a Indian enclaves in Leicester are dilute when compared to Chicago's black ghettos: the proportion of black Chicagoans and Indians in Leicester living in neighbourhoods with given proportions of their own ethnic group

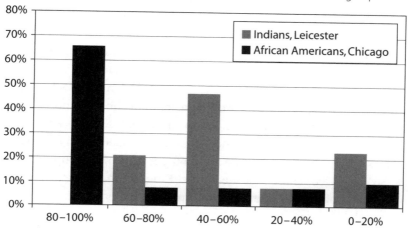

Figure 3.7b England also looks well assimilated when Bradford's Pakistanis are compared to African Americans in Miami

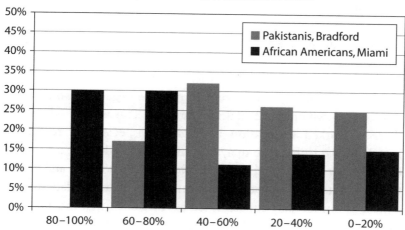

Source: All figures calculated from Peach (2009).

to that of Indians in Leicester and Pakistanis in Bradford. Minority ethnic individuals are bracketed according to the proportion of their neighbourhood that is made up by *their own ethnic group*. The great majority of African Americans in Chicago (66 per cent) live in places where they constitute over 80 per cent of the population. There are, however, no such wards within Leicester, and the plurality of Indians live in districts where they constitute around half (40 per cent to 60 per cent) of the population. A significant chunk also live in wards where Indians constitute only a small minority (20 per cent or less of the population), giving the community an outreach beyond its own enclave, something black people in Chicago may lack. As in Chicago, the great bulk of African Americans in Miami live in places where they constitute 60 per cent or more of the neighbourhood – almost a third living in places where they make up more than 80 per cent of the population. But in Bradford more than four Pakistanis in five live in places where they number less than 60 per cent of the population.

So can we conclude that the United Kingdom has no true ghettos at all? Not quite. Northern Ireland provides the one true exception, where ghettoisation is on religious rather than racial grounds. In Belfast, for instance, the clear majority (57 per cent) of Catholics live in wards where Catholics constitute over 80 per cent of the population, a reality unchanged even since cross-community violence has declined.[22] That represents comparable concentration to that for African Americans in Miami. Intriguingly, like African Americans, Ulster's Catholics are a native minority, suggesting that in the UK – just as in America – the densest ghettos are about something other than immigration.

Putting the special case of Ulster to one side, however, we have seen that African Americans remain more segregated than all other minorities – whether in Britain or America. This is not to deny that there is marked segregation in England, especially in respect of Bangladeshis. Nor is it to deny that this might indeed be a concern, just as Trevor Phillips argued. But despite his lively polemic, and despite the fact that when considered nationwide British Bangladeshis are almost as residentially concentrated as African Americans, there are no local enclaves of English Bangladeshis which match the intensity of the big African American ghettos. The remainder of this chapter relates these findings concerning its intensity to contrasting evidence

---

[22]Indeed, the ghettos have been given formal recognition and their boundary walls have been landscaped (Boal, 1995).

on the nature of segregation – and its bearing upon life chances – on the two sides of the Atlantic.

Monasteries and prisons: the nature of segregation

There is all the difference in the world between being forced to live apart and choosing to do so – just think of the contrast between a prison and a monastery. Before exploring the effect of the residential segregation we have uncovered in both Britain and America, we need first to pause and consider whether it is voluntary or instead somehow enforced.

Ethnic clustering is not necessarily bad news. It could, conceivably, foster a closer community (an argument we will consider further in Chapter 5), and bring advantages in terms of financial and other support networks that may outweigh the undoubted costs of living away from the mainstream. Certain small but highly segregated minorities on both sides of the Atlantic do indeed show that living in a *voluntary* enclave need not bring disadvantage. The Jewish community in London, for instance, is relatively prosperous, and yet highly segregated, with a 2001 ward-level ID score of 0.61, which is almost identical to that of Bangladeshi Muslims (Peach, 2006).[23] The bar on collecting official faith data prevents us doing the same calculation in the US, but similar calculations in Canada suggest that the similarly prosperous North American Jewish community may be even more segregated (Peach, 2005). Then there are groups such as the Amish community in Lancaster County, Pennsylvania who chose to set themselves apart in all sorts of ways and yet have demonstrated that such separation is compatible with successful social organisation.

Whatever advantages enclaves may foster, however, are likely to disappear when segregation is not chosen, but imposed. Trapped individuals who see no hope of rising *with* their community, and dream only of rising from it, will feel atomised, and will experience

---

[23]Jewish segregation in London, however, is of a rather different character from Bangladeshi segregation. Their high ID score is the product of their absence from many areas of London rather than their domination of their north London enclave. The highest proportion that Jews formed of any London ward was 37 per cent.

all interactions as zero-sum games – just as was described in Ley's (1974) classic account of Philadelphia's ghetto. The logic of atomisation is obviously destructive of trust, and once it is at work within a ghetto, the costs of living apart from the majority will not be compensated for, but will instead be compounded.

Both Britain and America are mercifully free of South African-style apartheid laws, so ghettos are not currently *legally* enforced in either. Whatever the law says, though, it hardly makes sense to regard ghettos as voluntary if those who live in them would prefer that they did not. History, poverty and – just as importantly – the attitudes of the majority may condemn certain races to live a life set apart. And in America at least, there are survey data to test the attitudes of different racial groups to mixing and segregation.

A pioneering study in the racially polarised environment of 1970s Detroit – a city which, three decades on, the census bureau ranks as America's most segregated[24] – asked people of different races about their willingness to live in neighbourhoods with different ethnic mixes (Farley *et al.*, 1978). It found that whites generally preferred to live apart from blacks: the overwhelming majority said they would leave a majority-black neighbourhood, and fully 40 per cent would leave one which was even one-third black. In sharp contrast, blacks showed a clear preference for mixed neighbourhoods – they saw the most desirable neighbourhood as one which was mixed between blacks and whites to an equal extent, conditions that we have seen few African Americans actually live in.

Now, 1970s Detroit was a highly distinctive case because of the severe social scarring left by that city's deadly race riots of 1967. The more general pattern found in American research, and in more recent decades within Detroit itself, has been that *most* white people are happy to live in a neighbourhood alongside *some* blacks, just as long as the black element does not grow too large. There is a consistent reluctance on the part of whites to live in neighbourhoods that are more than about 20 per cent African American (Farley *et al.*, 1994). Black people, by contrast, overwhelmingly continue to prefer a more equal racial

---

[24]Official rankings from 2002, cited in Taylor and Morin (2008).

split.[25] The consequence of this asymmetry in preferences for mixing can be to render mixed neighbourhoods dynamically unstable.

Imagine, for instance, that a certain proportion of whites are content to live among a community that is 15 per cent to 20 per cent black but becomes uneasy above that level. When the proportion of black families in a neighbourhood exceeds, say, 15 per cent, some whites may start to move out in search of a less diverse neighbourhood; at the same time more black people may move in precisely because the community is coming closer to the 50–50 mixing that they would typically prefer. But as the black population proportion creeps up to 25 per cent or 30 per cent, further whites may take flight if they feel the neighbourhood is getting too mixed for their own comfort. That would, once again, increase the black proportion of the population, setting in train a spiral of white flight and perhaps ultimately the creation of an all-black ghetto which black people themselves would not choose.[26] Indeed, evidence that the asymmetry of preferences can cause neighbourhoods undergoing racial transition to slide towards being almost all non-white, with dangerous consequences, has been found in practice.[27] Thus despite the fact that few blacks would choose to live in ghettos, the interaction of white and black preferences can produce them.

Mixed neighbourhoods suddenly become much more sustainable, though, when whites become less sensitive to race – which, on the face of it, is what has been happening. Surveys akin to the 1970s Detroit study carried out in 1990s America (summarised in Charles, 2003) have mostly found American whites becoming gradually more tolerant. One provocative new study, however, calls into question whether the apparent new tolerance is genuine, and observes that – even when survey responses are taken at face value – whites remain 23 percentage points less likely than blacks to express a preference for a racially mixed neighbourhood (Taylor and Morin, 2008). Besides,

[25]The 2004 Gallup poll, for instance, found only 14 per cent of blacks would like to live in a mostly black neighbourhood (compared to 78 per cent who would prefer a mixed neighbourhood) whereas fully 40 per cent of whites would explicitly prefer a mostly white neighbourhood (Gallup and Newport, 2004, p. 282).

[26]For more on the theory of how the asymmetry of preferences can give rise to tipping points within neighbourhoods even if individuals are not racist, see Schelling (1971) and Schelling (1978), pp. 137–166.

[27]See Vandell (1981).

the relatively recent research collated by Charles (2003) confirms the
continuing place of African Americans at the bottom of the pile: whites
are more tolerant about the prospect of Hispanic and Asian than black
neighbours, while Asians and Hispanics – who in general hanker after
integration – cool on the idea when the proposed integration is with
blacks. Another experiment (Charles, 2000) confirms that all non-
black groups regard blacks as the least desirable neighbours, and that
African Americans themselves are much less inclined to want to 'live
with their own kind' than any other racial group.

All of this – and the last finding in particular – strongly suggests
that the marked segregation of African Americans is a largely invol-
untary phenomenon. We are not aware of exactly comparable surveys
specifically in the UK, although one recent analysis discerns tentative signs of white flight using census data (Dorling and Rees, 2003)
and there is no reason in theory why it should not operate in the
UK as well, particularly because pan-European research discerns
a marked reluctance on the part of many whites to live alongside
largely minority ethnic populations (Semyonov et al., 2007). But there
is, nonetheless, reason to suspect that British residential segregation
is somewhat different in kind.

Take British Bangladeshis, who we have seen are almost as segregated as African Americans when viewed at the nationwide level. Most
African Americans would prefer integration, but that is unlikely to
be true of those Bangladeshi traditionalists who see it as desirable
to keep unmarried women away from British society. Of course, not
all Bangladeshis adopt such a view, and no doubt the clustering of
Bangladeshis in poor areas, such as Tower Hamlets in East London,
is partly a question of poverty. For African Americans, however, poverty
traditionally explains only a small proportion of segregation, a proportion estimated at just 12 per cent by one study (Taeuber and Taeuber,
1964). While they are the most segregated American minority, African
Americans are not the poorest, and in northern metropolitan areas
high-income blacks are similarly segregated from their white counterparts as poor blacks are from poor whites (Massey and Denton,
1993, p. 87). Even though America now has a sizeable black middle-
class that is quite unmatched among British Bangladeshis, African
Americans in the US thus still experience segregation to a greater extent.

Institutions turn out to be the key to resolving this apparent mystery. In America they worked to reinforce the dynamics of segregation that flow from asymmetric racial preferences for mixing; in the UK, they have worked to suppress them. In centralised Britain, after the ban on outright discrimination that was imposed during the 1960s, there were few practical bars on assimilation – despite widespread continuing racism. The landlords' signs saying 'no dogs, no blacks, and no Irish' were torn down, and ethnic minorities gained full access to private rented housing as well as to subsidised council housing which had once been the preserve of the white working class.

In decentralised America, by contrast, states, counties and even district councils had long used a range of planning and other tools to keep black and white people apart, and not all of these were easy to tackle through federal intervention. New highways were sometimes created in part with a view to separating white from 'undesirable' black neighbourhoods – Birmingham, Alabama's interstate highway system, for instance, attempted to maintain the racial boundaries which had been established by the city's 1926 racial zoning law. Social housing is relatively rare in the States, but many of the so-called projects were tightly targeted at providing accommodation in black neighbourhoods, and thus – whatever the intention – worked to keep African Americans in their ghetto. Often the intention was explicit. In cities such as Boston, public housing schemes were racialised, with black families steered towards black projects, and white families towards white projects.

Most important of all, however, were the mortgage providers, which the government supported through the Federal Housing Association. Its 1938 Underwriting Manual suggested that lenders should restrict loans for 'properties except by the race for which they are intended', not least because of the potential effect of mixing 'inharmonious racial groups' on local schooling. Such thinking may have seemed unexceptional at a time when all facilities in the South remained firmly segregated, but the legacy of this particular bit of institutionalised racism was to prove especially pronounced. With many African Americans being denied mortgages right through to the 1960s, the finance system effectively denied them the chance to move into white districts, imprisoning them in the ghetto. By the time such practices were outlawed, ghettos were so concentrated that few whites wanted to move in. Even today, the modest progress that has been made towards desegregation has come about more by black people moving out from the ghetto and into mixed neighbourhoods. There is no sign at all of mixing in the remaining overwhelmingly black districts.

Nonetheless, as Lyndon Johnson's so-called Great Society programme of legislation worked its way through, overall progress towards assimilation was eventually made. Despite the stubborn persistence of ghettos in several big cities, every census since 1970 has recorded that – across the US as a whole – the segregation of African Americans is on the decline, a trend which only underlines how important the previous institutional bars on integration were. We have discovered that the peculiar quantitative intensity of African American residential segregation is matched by a qualitative difference – black segregation in America was proactively imposed. Whereas economics has a role in British segregation, in the US the main drivers have historically been political. In the final section of this chapter we consider how these differences in the nature of segregation come to bear on other aspects of the lives of minorities.

Separate but unequal

The links between where people live and how they live are manifold. Groups that tend to live alone, cut off from the white majority, will use public services in which the majority have no stake, something that can affect the quality of hospitals and schools. More obviously, minorities that cluster away from the mainstream are less likely to have the chance to make friends or find partners within it. Drawing heavily on Waters (2009) we can summarise the main lessons of the scholarly evidence on how migrants and minorities live.

It is no surprise to learn that those communities whose homes are most segregated are also the least likely to marry outside their own ethnic group. Thus in the US, African Americans, the most segregated group, also marry outside their own group least. Barely one black woman in 40 (2.7 per cent) reports having a white husband. For Hispanics and Asians, by contrast, the ratio is one in five or more.

Another demographic axiom is that later generations of immigrants – who are typically less residentially segregated than their parents – also marry outside their own community more often. For both Hispanic and Chinese women born in America, the out-marriage rate is far greater than it is for the first generation. But despite this over-all tendency for immigrants to assimilate, differences in out-marriage rates *between* migrant groups show once again how salient the colour divide remains in American society. Black Caribbean immigrants in the US are on average more educated than African Americans, but once this is allowed for, they marry whites just as rarely.

In Britain, by contrast, just as we found with residential segregation, when it comes to marriage a great deal seems to depend on the culture of the community in question – and black Caribbeans turn out to be the community that out-marries the most. One Afro-Caribbean man in three partners outside his own group,[28] an established pattern which gives rise to a sizeable group of mixed race offspring, who overwhelmingly go on to partner into the white majority. Integration is proceeding so rapidly for Britain's Afro-Caribbean population that one scholar suggests that within three generations the black–white divide might cease to bear on patterns of marriage at all (Patterson, 2005). Just like America's melting pot, however, the British cauldron bubbles away at very different speeds for different minorities. We have seen that Bangladeshis are the most segregated of Britain's minorities, and it is no coincidence that they also out-marry least – partnering with whites even less frequently than African Americans do.

Because segregation affects who members of a group associate with, it can also affect lifestyle and, through that, everything from the chances of getting sick to the chances of ending up on the wrong side of the law. We have seen that most American immigrants amalgamate into society relatively rapidly, and the sense that this is beneficial is confirmed by the fact that immigrants are relatively unlikely to wind up in jail. America's federal prison structure clouds its prison statistics, but one British source that collates international data puts the

---

[28]Figure from Peach (2009). Unfortunately UK data are for 'partnership' whereas the American data are for marriage, although the two concepts are close enough to allow meaningful comparison.

total proportion of foreigners in America's jails at a mere 5.8 per cent; less than half the overall population proportion that is born overseas.[29] Indeed, several scholarly studies have examined the link between immigration and low crime (see, for example, Martinez and Valenzuela, 2006, or Hagan and Palloni, 1999). In sharp contrast, around 14 per cent of prisoners in England and Wales were born overseas,[30] which is *nearly double* the proportion of the foreign-born in the British population as a whole.

When it comes to race, however, black people are similarly over-represented in proportional terms in both Britain and the US,[31] and because incarceration remains much more common in America, this particular race divide is of much more absolute importance there. The criminal justice system, then, provides fresh evidence that the race divide seems more marked in America, while the difficulties of immigrants seem more pronounced in Britain.

Looking at health, similar patterns emerge. Migrants once again fare well in the US. Indeed, American immigrants enjoy a premium of some 3.4 years in life expectancy when compared to natives (Adler and Rehkopf, 2008). American scholars have debated whether this might reflect the effect of migration, data problems or – perfectly plausibly – the tendency among healthier individuals to embark on relocating in the first place. The difficulty with this last suggestion, however, is that there is no such effect within the UK – the main British immigrant groups report significantly worse health than the white majority (Nazroo, 2003). Once again, then, transatlantic comparisons suggest that Britain has lessons to learn from America when it comes to assimilating immigrants. Again, however, when it comes to the heavily segregated African Americans, the situation in

[29]Figures collated by the International Centre for Prison Studies at King's College, London. Available at: www.kcl.ac.uk/depsta/law/research/icps/worldbrief/wpb_stats.php?area=northam&category=wb_foreign

[30]Official figures, available at: www.justice.gov.uk/docs/omcs2007.pdf

[31]The 2007 official figures for England and Wales are available at www.justice.gov.uk/docs/omcs2007.pdf. Table 7.21 suggests blacks made up 15 per cent of the prison population, whereas the census suggests that blacks constitute a little over 3 per cent of England and Wales's population. US Department for Justice figures for year-end 2002 are available at www.ojp.usdoj.gov/bjs/pub/pdf/p02.pdf. Table 13 suggests that blacks constitute 45 per cent of the sentenced prison population compared to around 13 per cent of the total population.

the US is markedly depressing. Official figures show that blacks in America live five years less, a gap so large that it compares to the widely appreciated difference in lifespan between men and women.[32]

In the British data, there is some correspondence between patterns of social and economic inequalities and patterns of residential segregation, in that the highly segregated Bangladeshis and Pakistanis also suffer, for instance, from worse health. But making a definitive causal connection is tricky – because some underlying factors, such as poverty, could lie behind both segregation and other problems, such as poorer health. In education, however, the links between being separate and being unequal have been explored much more methodically, through controlling for all sorts of characteristics. In the US, Card and Rothstein (2007) find that higher segregation widens the grade gap between black and white students. Shifting from a highly segregated city to a nearly integrated one removes about a quarter of the raw racial difference in attainment; powerful fresh evidence that African American ghettos do disadvantage their residents. Similar new analysis for the UK, in sharp contrast, suggests that the test score deficit affecting some ethnic groups of schoolchildren, such as Pakistanis and Caribbeans, is 'largely unaffected by segregation' (Burgess *et al.*, 2008).

This new research on education reinforces one of the central arguments of this chapter – that the uniquely intense African American ghetto is more pernicious than the racial segregation found within the UK. It is important to remember, however, that segregation is very far from being the only factor to bear on educational and other opportunities – all sorts of other things matter, including the language barriers, the relative affluence and the culture of learning found within each particular community. Figures 3.8a and 3.8b use census data to show how the education system as a whole ultimately 'cashes in' for pupils of different races, by charting the proportion of women in the main ethnic groups to have secured education at the tertiary level – which includes both college graduate and other post-high school qualifications – in both Britain and the US. Intriguingly, in

[32]See: www.cdc.gov/nchs/products/pubs/pubd/hestats/prelimdeaths04/preliminarydeaths04.htm

Figure 3.8a Proportion of women from different ethnic groups with 'tertiary' education in the UK

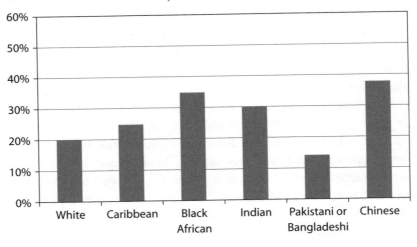

Figure 3.8b Proportion of women from different ethnic groups with 'tertiary' education in the US

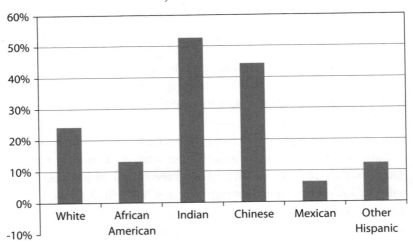

Source: Calculated by Li (2009) using census data.
Note: Tertiary education is defined to include both college education and successful completion of professional and other qualifications that are above the level of mandatory schooling.

both countries the charts suggest that whites are something of an average group. In the US, white women are far more qualified than the largest minority groups (African Americans, Mexicans and other Hispanics), but are far less so than Indian or Chinese women. In Britain, meanwhile, white women outperform Pakistanis and Bangladeshis, but lag well behind both their Chinese and Indian counterparts.

Results for men, available in Li (2009), show some differences compered with the results for women. For example, in the UK, Pakistani men do relatively better than Pakistani women, while Caribbean men do relatively worse. However, the similarities between the genders are more notable – with huge variation in the educational attainment across ethnic groups, and with whites remaining something of an average group in both countries.

This chapter has established that many immigrant communities have assimilated into the US mainstream much more successfully than the indigenous black population – not only in terms of residential integration, but also on all sorts of indicators ranging from health to education. In Britain, several groups of immigrants do face difficulties, but fortunes vary greatly between them. The mixed picture that emerged in terms of residential integration – with Caribbeans assimilated, Bangladeshis set apart, and Indians somewhere in between – does not relate straightforwardly to educational performance, as Indians outperform not only these other minorities, but also the white majority. The next chapter asks how far these complex patterns of advantage and disadvantage carry over into the world of work.

For the most part, this chapter has shown that segregation is not only marked but that, particularly in the US, it tends to be associated with disadvantage. This need not always be the case, however. We will revisit the complex impact of ethnic clustering on community life in Chapter 5 and then, in Chapter 7, we will consider one potential advantage of segregation that we have not yet touched on – namely, its potential to provide ethnic minorities with a political power base. As we will see, the very concentration of African Americans fostered the creation of a black political class, a class whose existence blazed the trail for President Obama.

4

The rickety ladder of opportunity: minorities and work

'Everything's free in America', the Puerto Ricans sing in *West Side Story*, before adding: 'for a small fee in America'. The hope of a better life is, of course, what draws immigrants to the rich world. But making good on that hope very often depends on money, and the means to earn it. This chapter examines the prospects that minorities have of finding work, and of finding good work in particular. Some poor new-comers, resigned to hardship themselves, nonetheless dream that their children might one day do better, and live a more comfortable life. Like their own fortunes, however, such dreams live or die in the labour market. We will thus keep an eye out for signs of rising social mobility across the generations.

Our analysis uses the most authoritative available source in both countries: the national census. For both countries, we have samples from the last two such compulsory surveys – 1991 and 2001 in Britain, and 1990 and 2000 for the US.[33] Together, they contain literally millions of records, giving us enough detailed data to pass confident judgement not just on how minorities fare compared to the white majority, but on how the prospects of getting ahead in the workplace vary *between* different minority groups.

[33]The 2 per cent Sample of Anonymised Records (SAR) of the 1991 Census of Population and the 3 per cent SAR of the 2001 Census of Population for Great Britain. For the US, the 1 per cent Integrated Public Use Microdata Series (IPUM), for both 1990 and 2000.

Finding a job is a job in itself

The first and most obvious question is: who gets the jobs? The immediate answer provided by the last census in both countries is, more or less, that white people are always and everywhere more likely to be in work. Figures 4.1a and 4.1b show the unemployment rates for men in the three biggest minority ethnic groups in 2001 Britain and 2000 America – and in both countries the whites have less unemployment than the others, indeed substantially less.

Most of the bars for minorities are higher in Britain than the US. This reflects different rates of overall male unemployment – measured as slightly higher in the British census sample (5.3 per cent) than in the American data (4.5 per cent) – and so does not tell us anything about relative disadvantage. Homing in on the differences between the bars, though, we can see that African Americans are a little more than twice as likely to be out of work as white Americans, the same sort of ratio as is found between Pakistani-Bangladeshis and the white majority in Britain. Aside from African Americans, however, the biggest American minorities fare reasonably well by British standards. Although much more likely than whites to be unemployed, both Mexicans and 'other Hispanics' are considerably less than twice as likely to be so, unlike Pakistani-Bangladeshis or Black Caribbeans in Britain, both of whom are much more than twice as likely to be unemployed as whites.

Interestingly, *if* these charts are evidence of anti-minority discrimination in the jobs market, then they also suggest that white prejudice does not operate in an even-handed way. The differences between the unemployment rates of different minorities – for example between low-unemployment Indians and high-unemployment Caribbeans in Britain – are sometimes greater than the excess unemployment of minorities as a whole over that of the white majority. Add in those smaller minorities, not shown on the chart, and the variation becomes even starker. Chinese men, for instance, are actually *less* likely than whites to be unemployed in either country – with an unemployment rate of 4.8 per cent in Britain and just 2.7 per cent in the US.

There are many reasons for being without work besides being unemployed – among them disability, child-rearing and other caring responsibilities. These barriers to work, however, can often be

Figure 4.1a Men from the main minorities suffer from more
unemployment in Britain...

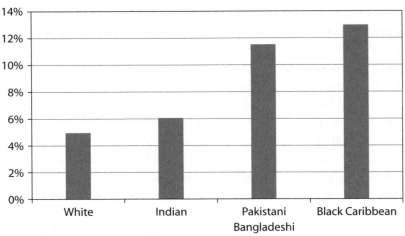

Figure 4.1b ...just like men from the main American minorities

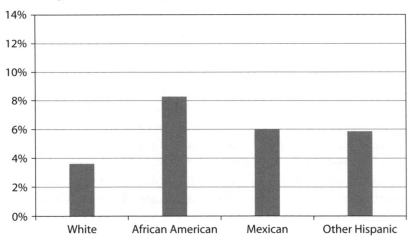

Sources: 3 per cent Sample of Anonymised Records from the 2001 British census. 1 per cent
IPUM sample from the 2000 American census.
Note: Percentage of men aged 16–64 in each selected ethnic group identified as unemployed.

overcome with the right support. There are other jobless people who
are not counted as unemployed, simply because they have grown dis-
couraged and so ceased to look for work. Thus it is important to look
at the overall employment rate, as well as unemployment. This is shown

for our main minority groups in Figures 4.2a and 4.2b, though this time we concentrate on women.

On this gauge, once again minorities are revealed to be at a disadvantage, with each of the main groups of minority women less likely

Figure 4.2a Women from the main minorities are less likely than whites to have a job in Britain...

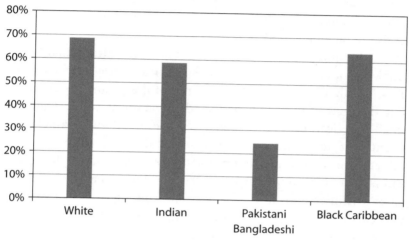

Figure 4.2b ...and the same is true of women from American minorities

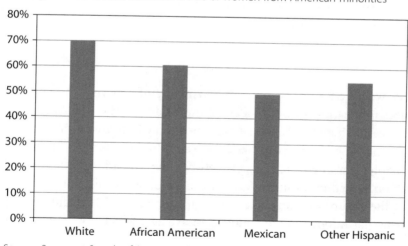

Sources: 3 per cent Sample of Anonymised Records from the 2001 British census. 1 per cent IPUM sample from the 2000 American census.
Note: Percentage of women aged 16–59 in each selected ethnic group who are in employment.

to be in work than their white counterparts. That headline is very much in line with Figures 4.1a and 4.1b, but a very different picture of inter-minority comparisons emerges this time round. In stark contrast to the results for male unemployment, we see both Caribbean British women and African Americans doing relatively well compared to other minorities. Among men, both these groups have low employment rates,[34] so this turnaround reflects an intra-minority gender differential, rather than the shift from the unemployment to the employment yardstick.

One bar jumps out among all the others: the extraordinarily low employment rate (24.4 per cent) for Pakistani and Bangladeshi women. This is both a cause and a consequence of this group's deprivation. But there are also factors besides deprivation at work. The very small American Pakistani-Bangladeshi community is strikingly different from its British counterpart – it is far more affluent, and is actually over-represented among the professions – and yet the census shows that this community, too, has an exceptionally low female employment rate, of just 41.1 per cent. This suggests that the low participation rate among Pakistani and Bangladeshi women is not just a question of deprivation but a cultural phenomenon, possibly reflecting concerns about exposing these women to a corrupting Western society, and linked to the tendency discussed in the last chapter for these minorities to live apart.

Getting to grips with the gap

So, we have found a gaping employment gulf between white people and minorities on both sides of the Atlantic. The next questions concern whether this can be explained away in terms of the characteristics of minority members. For example, we have seen in the last chapter that there are big gaps between the educational attainments of various ethnic groups – how far can the poor qualifications of some of the groups explain the ethnic employment gap? It might also be true that minorities are younger on average, which could also have

---

[34]In our data, 63.9 per cent of British Black Caribbeans in 2001 and just 55.9 per cent of African Americans in 2000 were employed.

an effect, as could any tendency for them to have more children. We can unpick all of this, using statistical tests ('regressions') which allow us to estimate the strength of the link between the thing we are interested in (employment) and the factor we are most interested in (ethnicity) while holding other factors constant.

As well as race, the personal attributes we 'control for' include age,[35] and whether or not the individual has a tertiary-level qualification, a partner, dependent children or a long-term illness. We also allow for the possibility that each factor may bear on different minorities in different ways – for example, having children may be less of a drain on women's earnings within their community if the assumption is that mothers do not work; alternatively, it may be less of a disadvantage among groups where there is a strong tradition of extended family providing informal childcare.[36] Finally, we are interested in how far any 'ethnic penalty' is in fact a penalty paid by newcomers (which then fades), rather than one related to race (which endures). We can investigate that by splitting immigrants into first and subsequent generations, using 'country of birth' information from the census – with those born abroad classed as 'first generation' and those born within the UK and the US classed as 'second generation', although some of these will in fact be third or even higher generations.

Figure 4.3 shows the results – the predicted likelihood of being in a job for men in both the US and the UK. As well as first- and second-generation immigrant minorities, for the US we added a separate category for African Americans, who – having been settled in the US for longer than most white people – are not immigrants at all, but still face racial penalties. For each group, these likelihoods are expressed *as a percentage of the likelihood of white men in the same country being in work*. Thus for whites in both countries the figure is, by construction, 100 per cent.

Recall that we have controlled for education and other factors, so the percentages gauge how far the employment prospects for a

---

[35]We include both age and age squared. The latter allows for the possibility that the effect of age may be in a different direction for older and younger people.

[36]Such possibilities are referred to as 'interaction effects'; see Li (2009) for more details on the techniques deployed.

Figure 4.3 Minorities face a diminished chance of being in work compared to 'similar' white individuals

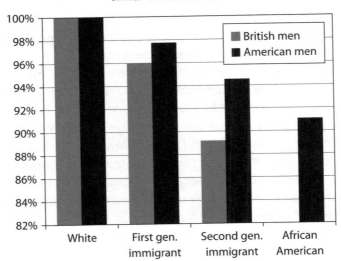

Sources: 3 per cent Sample of Anonymised Records from the 2001 British census. 1 per cent IPUM sample from the 2000 American census.
Notes: Likelihoods for individuals from each minority group are expressed as a percentage of the chance of a white man with similar characteristics being in work in the same country. Analysis is restricted to employed and unemployed individuals, as the reasons for economic inactivity are too diverse to ascertain using our data. 'First-generation immigrants' are minority ethnic individuals born abroad; 'second-generation immigrants' are minority ethnic individuals born within, respectively, Britain and the US.

minority individual are diminished when compared with *an otherwise-similar white person*. And – at least when minorities are divided up as they are on this chart – the prospect of working is always diminished. The figures for second-generation immigrants, for instance, are 94.5 per cent in America and 89.2 per cent in Britain. We call the shortfall below 100 the ethnic 'penalty', so these figures imply penalties on the prospect of working of between 5.5 and 10.8 percentage points. Thus even after having adjusted for differences in education and other factors that may vary between different ethnic groups, a substantial employment gap exists.

The adverse impact for both first- and second-generation immigrants is more marked – indeed it is almost twice as large – in Britain than it is in America. That might suggest that Britain is the less attractive place to settle. More troubling for the US, however, is the position of African Americans, who face none of the language barriers or problems of dislocation that may confront other immigrant minorities, but nonetheless face a larger employment gap. In line with our findings about ghettoisation in the previous chapter, this is another reminder of the special power of the black–white racial cleavage in American society.

Perhaps the least-expected result, in both Britain and the US, is that second-generation immigrants appear to pay a bigger penalty than their parents. Between the first and second generation, there is a *drop* in the likelihood of working relative to whites of 6.8 percentage points in Britain, and 3.3 points in the US. At first blush this appears as a damning indictment of both societies, suggesting that the children of immigrants are not so much offered a ladder of opportunity to climb, as a snake to slide down to the very bottom of the pile. An optimistic reading of this grim finding is, however, possible. Second-generation immigrants might have higher aspirations, and a little more financial security, and as a result might be less likely to be rushed into doing menial work. The last substantive section of this chapter, which deals with the *types* of job people do, sheds light on whether this is tenable.

For women, the results are strikingly similar to those displayed for men. The relative probabilities are in every case within three percentage points of those shown in Figure 4.3, and all the main contrasts stand up among females too. Just as with men, immigrant women fare relatively better in America than in Britain. In both countries, too, they appear to do better at the first than the second generation. And within the US, African American women – just like African American men – suffer a bigger employment penalty than immigrants.[37]

It is also possible to calculate employment penalties separately for individual minority ethnic groups (see Li (2009) for the full set of results) although this does not drastically change the picture either. Every minority group of British men at both the first and second generation continues to face an employment gap, although in the case of Indian and Chinese men this gap is considerably smaller than

[37]The full set of results can be found in Li (2009).

the average penalties shown in Figure 4.3, whereas for Pakistanis and Bangladeshis it is considerably larger. In America, by contrast, some minorities – most importantly the Chinese, but also the small but prosperous Indian and Pakistani-Bangladeshi populations – enjoy a very modest employment *premium*; that is, they are actually more likely to be in work than whites, by around one percentage point. With Indians and Pakistani-Bangladeshis, however, the premium is purely a first-generation phenomenon, which might arise, for instance, if many new immigrants arrived in response to the offer of a particular job. For all the more numerous minorities – such as Mexicans and other Hispanics – the penalties are much in line with those in Figure 4.3.

A final question is whether the pattern of penalties is ameliorating over time. Li (2009) compares the 2001 and 1991 censuses, a comparison which initially suggests that things are indeed getting much better in the UK – declining, for example, for second-generation immigrant women from 22.9 to 7.8 percentage points. This improvement *could* be genuine. It could, however, be a product of the economic cycle: in 1991 the UK was in the trough of a major recession, which saw the unemployment rate almost double, whereas in 2001 the economy was buoyant. If, for instance, minority ethnic workers are always the first to get laid off in a slump, then their employment rate will be 'hyper-cyclical',[38] with penalties inflated during slumps and depressed during periods of prosperity. As we enter the throes of a new recession, this is not a heartening thought. In America, where overall unemployment was broadly comparable in the two census years 1990 and 2000, the results for the two dates are virtually indistinguishable, suggesting there is no strong underlying current pushing towards greater fairness.[39]

For most immigrants and minorities, then, the first crucial rung on the ladder of economic opportunity – the step into work – is decidedly rickety. We now turn to consider whether the higher rungs, those

---

[38]Cheung and Heath (2007).

[39]For both men and women, relative predicted probabilities of being in employment for African Americans and first- and second-generation immigrants are within a percentage point of those in 2000. Full set of results in Li (2009).

that step up into the middle class and the professions, are any more robust.

Class action

The dreams of most immigrants do not involve being stuck in dead-end work. Having established who gets jobs in the first place, the second, and more interesting, question is: who gets the best jobs? Naturally, people differ about what counts as a 'good job', but on most people's list would be decent pay, security and working conditions, as well as some measure of autonomy. All of these things are associated with the professional and managerial middle-class posts that we bracket together and label as 'salariat'.[40] The censuses give enough information to allow us to pick out such jobs with reasonable consistency on the two sides of the Atlantic.[41]

Figure 4.4 shows how this picture varies for men of different ethnic groups across the two countries. (We concentrate chiefly on men in this section partly for methodological reasons.)[42] Across the male labour force, 40 per cent of white Britons held salariat positions in 2001; not so different from the 36.8 per cent figure recorded for the United States of 2000. But the striking thing about the chart is just how much variety there is. With employment, in Figures 4.1a and b and 4.2a and b, we restricted ourselves to the few largest ethnic groups because the more detailed analysis suggested that adding more groups would

[40]This 'salariat' class is the top tranche of the best-known 'Goldthorpe schema', with the lower two classes being 'intermediate' (e.g. office clerks, forepersons, skilled workers and small employers) and 'routine' (e.g. labourers and lower-grade personal service workers). See Goldthorpe *et al.* (1987).

[41]Li (2009) gives more details and further references on how this is derived from the official census class schemas for the UK, which changed between 1991 and 2001. For the US, the starting point is the standard occupational classification variable, *occ1990*, but lower managerial and higher supervisorial personnel are shifted into the top 'salariat' tier for consistency with the British data.

[42]In the regression analysis that follows – like that for employment above – we have had to exclude the economically inactive, as the reasons for their inactivity are too varied to be unpicked using census data. This affects the figures for women more than those for men because more women are 'inactive'. In addition, the occupational class of men arguably retains a particular bearing on the class position of families because in both Britain and the US men retain much greater earning power.

Figure 4.4 Huge variation in the number of men employed
in salariat professions

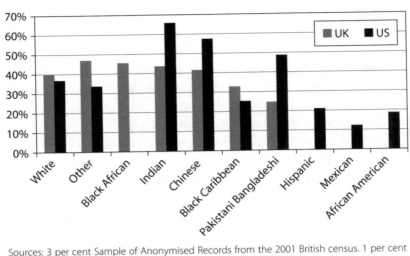

Sources: 3 per cent Sample of Anonymised Records from the 2001 British census. 1 per cent
IPUM sample from the 2000 American census.
Note: Percentage of men aged 16–64 who are in work in each ethnic group whose
occupation is classed as 'salariat'.

not much change the main story: whites were more likely to work
than minorities. When it comes to working in salariat professions,
though, while some minorities continue to fare very badly, members
of several others – the chart suggests – are much more likely to get
lucky than white individuals.

For some smaller minorities, take Indians in the US for example,
the difference is huge – 65.8 per cent of South Asian Indian men in
the American workforce are in the salariat, compared to just 36.8 per
cent of their white counterparts. But even for some proportionally
more significant minorities, there is an appreciable and positive difference. Of Chinese men in the American workforce, for instance,
57.8 per cent are classified as salariat. In Britain, where Indians are
the biggest single minority, the chart shows that 43.7 per cent are in
these professions, against just 40.1 per cent for whites. Among the
rapidly growing band of Black Africans, the figure is even higher, at
45.4 per cent.

At the same time, however, other minorities seem to fare extraordinarily badly – most particularly, the three biggest minority

groups in the US. Salariat access for Hispanics (21 per cent), African Americans (18.7 per cent) and – most particularly – Mexicans (12.4 per cent) is appallingly low. In the UK, Afro-Caribbeans and Pakistani-Bangladeshis lag way behind whites, albeit to a somewhat lesser extent.

Looked at in proportional terms, the differences are even more shocking. Indian men in the US are fully five times as likely – 530 per cent as likely to be exact – to make it to salariat professions as Mexicans. It seems highly unlikely that such discrepancies could be down to differences in drive or motivation between people from different communities. On the face of it, a race gap besets the top jobs on both sides of the Atlantic, a gap that renders political rhetoric about equal life chances utterly hollow.

But are the apparently shocking differences really what they seem? They would certainly be hard to explain through a crude story of racism alone – the big disadvantage facing Pakistanis in Britain, after all, comes alongside an apparent premium on promotion prospects for phenotypically similar Indians. Maybe we can explain the big differences away by taking other things into account. Education is, after all, supposed to be the key to the professions – perhaps differences in access to plum jobs by ethnic group do not reflect prejudice in the labour market, but differences in qualifications instead. Recall that the last chapter showed some very big racial differences in educational attainment.

We can investigate this using the same sort of regression analysis deployed to 'control for' education in considering employment penalties in the previous section. Along with education (whether or not the individual has a tertiary-level qualification), we again factor in various other characteristics that could also affect the chance of promotion – age,[43] having a partner, having dependent children or having a long-term illness. This time, however, because the inter-ethnic variations are so stark, we begin by analysing the effect on different minorities separately, rather than lumping them all together as first- or second-generation immigrants.

---

[43]Including, once again, separate age and age-squared terms.

Figures 4.5a and 4.5b chart the results. They show the relative likelihood of being in a salariat job for men in selected minorities, expressed *as a percentage of the likelihood of an otherwise-similar white man being in the salariat.* The figures for whites are thus always 100 per cent. Even after allowing for education and the rest, it appears that significant ethnic variations remain, particularly in the US where the spread of likelihoods is spectacular.

The variation between the British bars is perhaps somewhat less marked this time than it was before we controlled for education in Figure 4.4. Nonetheless, the differences remain substantial. As we saw in the last chapter, African and Indian men are more likely to have tertiary education than the average white Briton. But even allowing for this, they retain a modest premium in accessing the salariat – at both the first and the second generation. Taking second-generation Indian men as an example, their chance of reaching the salaried station in life is shown as 112 per cent, a premium of 12 percentage points. Black Caribbeans and Pakistani-Bangladeshis, by contrast, both start out with poorer qualifications, but even once we strip that out, further disadvantage remains. For first-generation Pakistani-Bangladeshis, in particular, it remains extraordinarily marked – with the chart recording a figure of 52 per cent, a penalty of 48 percentage points. In sum, allowing for *individual* education explains only *part* of the difference between communities, suggesting perhaps that there might be an advantage – whatever one's own level of education – in coming from a more educated community. When address books are as important for getting jobs as qualifications, that seems highly plausible.

In America, inter-ethnic differences still seem as marked as they were before controlling for education, and the rank-ordering between the minorities is barely changed at all. We may again be seeing an *address-book effect* – with community contacts trumping qualifications – but this time an even more powerful one. Indians, once again, have the best prospects, which for the first generation are recorded as being 185 per cent of those for whites, i.e. a premium of 85 percentage points. The Chinese follow close behind, with a premium of 59 points, which rises to 65 points in the second generation. Mexicans and Hispanics continue to do severely badly, particularly in the first

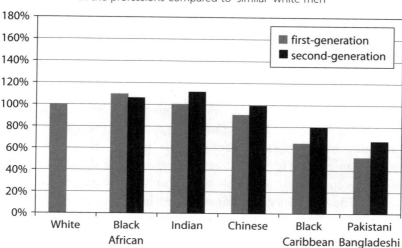

Figure 4.5a Men from British minorities face a variable chance of being in the professions compared to 'similar' white men

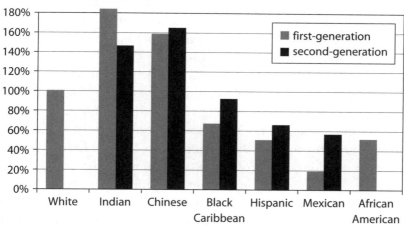

Figure 4.5b The prospects of American men are even more diverse

Sources: 3 per cent Sample of Anonymised Records from the 2001 British census. 1 per cent IPUM sample from the 2000 American census.

Notes: Likelihoods for individuals from each minority group are expressed as a percentage of the chance of a white man with similar characteristics being in the 'salariat' in the same country. Not every minority group is shown. 'First-generation immigrants' are minority ethnic individuals born abroad; 'second-generation immigrants' are minority ethnic individuals born within, respectively, Britain and the US.

generation – where Mexicans suffer a penalty of an extraordinary 80 percentage points. That is to say, even if a first-generation Mexican immigrant is – in so far as our data can distinguish – exactly like a white individual in other respects, he nonetheless has only one-fifth of the chance of joining the ranks of the managers and professionals.

For such a Mexican newcomer, some of the obstacles to advancement – which are not directly visible in the census – are likely connected to a lack of roots and connections within America, and also potentially language. The second generation may be a fairer test of how migrants are treated, because such barriers are almost bound to have an effect. The salariat has been growing in the US (as it also has been in Britain) which should aid upward social mobility. But has it? The chart suggests that it has, with a big drop in the ethnic penalty for Mexicans at the second generation, where it has declined from 80 to 43 points. Indeed, on both sides of the Atlantic, across all those communities which start off facing a penalty, that penalty shrinks substantially – typically by around ten points in Britain, and by substantially more in the US – between the first and second generation, an encouraging sign of upward social mobility. African Americans, however, despite their effective status as 'natives', continue to lag behind. By the second generation, every immigrant group has overtaken them – each having a smaller penalty than the 48-point disadvantage for African Americans.

The picture might seem so varied as to defy any neat transatlantic comparison. Before concluding, it is thus worth looking at the picture again when taking all immigrants together – to give us a sense of how the 'average' minority fares within each country, as shown in Figure 4.6. This suggests that minorities in America have a tougher time in reaching the professions than those in Britain. For the average first-generation immigrant, the ethnic penalty in Britain is 10 percentage points, compared with 35 points in the US. The American picture now emerges as bleaker because of the preponderance of those immigrants – notably Mexicans and Hispanics – that face big ethnic penalties. In both countries the penalties again diminish at the second generation, implying that – on average – we are seeing upward social mobility, a heartening contrast to what we found with employment. In both countries there is a decline in penalties across

Figure 4.6 Men from American minorities typically face bigger penalties in reaching the professions than their counterparts in the UK

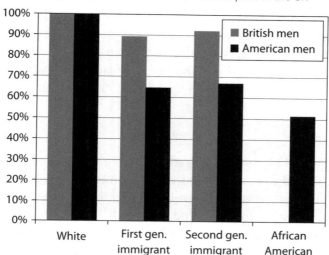

Sources: Three per cent Sample of Anonymised Records from the 2001 British census. One per cent IPUM sample from the 2000 American census.
Notes: Likelihoods for individuals from each minority group are expressed as a percentage of the chance of a white man with similar characteristics being in the 'salariat' in the same country. 'First-generation immigrants' are minority ethnic individuals born abroad; 'second-generation immigrants' are minority ethnic individuals born within, respectively, Britain and the US.

generations, around three percentage points in each case, which is – if anything – likely to be an underestimate of progress.[44] This encouraging finding suggests that the worrying apparent decline in overall second-generation employment that we previously found may reflect the aspirations and security of later cohorts in holding out for better jobs. The chart underlines once again, however, how African Americans continue to be left behind.

We have concentrated in this section on men, but Li (2009) provides similar analysis for women, and the picture is little changed. The only real difference is that the scale of upward mobility at the second generation is more marked – so marked in Britain that

[44]The bigger declines – often ten points or more – shown on the more differentiated Figures 4.5a and 4.5b might be more informative, since interpretation of the simplified Figure 4.6 is complicated by changes in the relative size of different minorities between the generations.

second-generation women end up with a modest premium over whites in terms of their chances of reaching the salariat. African American women also fare badly, and, more generally, immigrant penalties for women are on average bigger in the US than in Britain. Li (2009) also compares the results to those in 1990–91, and concludes that penalties have declined sharply in Britain, but – while tending to edge downwards – have remained much more stable in the US.

Conclusions

'They got cars big as bars, they got rivers of gold' was how the Pogues summed up the excitement of Irish newcomers to New York. But the excess unemployment endured by immigrants in both the US and the UK instead brings to mind the words of Bob Dylan – 'I pity the poor immigrant who wishes he would have stayed home'. That excess unemployment blights the lives of virtually all minorities, and it seems to do so more markedly in Britain than it does in the United States.

If America is the better place to get a first foot on the economic ladder, the position is reversed when it comes to clambering up it. Overall, migrants and minorities are less likely to attain plum middle-class jobs – and the security and status they bring – on both sides of the Atlantic, although the gap on this count is much more marked in America.

There are, however, encouraging signs that while most first-generation immigrants pay a lifelong ethnic penalty, the children of immigrants fare better at accessing desirable jobs. For most large British immigrant minority groups, the proportion achieving this rises markedly between the first and second generations; in America, meanwhile, Mexicans do spectacularly better than their parents.

This simple summary, however, compresses a rainbow into white light. There are many minorities, especially in America, that are much more likely than white people to wind their way into salariat professions. But there are many other groups – that are more demographically significant – which face stunted opportunities, even when they do succeed in getting themselves qualified. African Americans are foremost among them.

The most feasible interpretation of the ethnic penalties we have observed, however, is not crude racism – which could not explain the divergent prospects of phenotypically similar groups, such as Indians and Pakistani-Bangladeshis in Britain, in securing the top jobs. So there is something more complex going on. Different levels of education among the first wave of immigrants are no doubt part of the picture, as these differences are often passed on from one generation to another. But it also seems plausible that the social networks of immigrants' own communities are coming into play – those who come from groups that are more educated and better-connected on average can secure the better jobs. Community is, there is no doubt, a powerful thing. In the next chapter, we turn to consider how diversity may affect it – not just for minorities, but for everybody.

5

Mosaic or cracked vase?
Diversity and community life

If there were only one religion in England there would be danger of despotism, if there were two, they would cut each other's throats, but there are thirty, and they live in peace and happiness. (Voltaire, French thinker, writing in the first half of the eighteenth century)[45]

We share public services and parts of our income in the welfare state, we share public spaces in towns and cities where we are squashed together on buses, trains and tubes, and we share in a democratic conversation ... about the collective choices we wish to make. All such acts of sharing are more smoothly and generously negotiated if we can take for granted a limited set of common values and assumptions. But as Britain becomes more diverse that common culture is being eroded. (David Goodhart, British journalist, writing in 2004)[46]

Where does diversity lead society – towards enlightened co-existence, or mean-spirited fragmentation? Since Voltaire, at least, the question has been debated. Like all questions about diversity, however, it becomes more important as Western societies grow more heterogeneous. Voltaire's optimistic take on England's mosaic of religions contrasts with David Goodhart's anxiety about cultural unravelling in the wake of contemporary migration. In academic argument, each of these two perspectives has long had its counterpart, in theories of 'contact' on the one hand and of 'conflict' on the other.

Contact theorists (for instance, Allport, 1954) held that contact with other ethnic groups – more likely in a diverse society – will reduce racist attitudes. Conflict theorists on the other hand (for example,

---

[45]Voltaire (1980 [1734], p. 41).
[46]*Prospect*, 20 February 2004.

Blalock, 1967) have long reasoned that being brought close to those who belong to other groups encourages people to react with hostility. Whether out of some generalised fear of 'the other' or motivated by fear that one's group may lose control of some resource (such as social housing or the local council), under this account people respond to difference by 'sticking to their own'. A variant on the conflict hypothesis is that different ethnic communities may have different values, and may come to loggerheads by seeking to impose these upon one another. In the British context, this 'clash of cultures' account has received particular attention in connection with Islam.[47]

This chapter, however, is less concerned with assessing each of the different mechanisms through which diversity may potentially affect community than with assessing the aggregate effect. As well as assessing whether diversity tends to give rise more to conflict or to friendly contact in each of our countries, we will also – in a novel twist – evaluate its effect separately for whites and for minorities. Doing so sheds valuable new light on the nature of the diversity effect.

Measuring community health – enter 'social capital'

In recent years, the conflict–contact debate has often been played out through the concept of 'social capital' – which, in essence, is the value attached to social networks, and to those attitudes, such as trust, that go along with them. In this chapter, we will look at both elements – assessing the link between diversity in a locality on the one hand, and, on the other, how community-minded and communally active its citizens are.

The credit crunch has shown that financial capital on banks' balance sheets is often hard to measure, and – while the ties of neighbourhood, kith and kin are indubitably important – the social variety of capital is even harder to count. Increasingly, though, counting it is

---

[47]There is some survey evidence that Britain's Muslims are appreciably more conservative on a range of social issues – including homosexuality and pre-marital sex – than their compatriots; and indeed that the gap between non-Muslim and Muslim Britons is larger than the gap between Muslims and non-Muslims in comparable European countries. See, for instance, the Gallup survey reported in *The Economist* on 9 May 2009; available at: www.economist.com/world/britain/displaystory.cfm?story_id=13612116

exactly what scholars are doing. When they do so they find that it is strongly linked with everything from individual health and wealth through to self-reported contentment (Putnam, 2000; Halpern, 2005). The relationship between social capital and diversity might thus settle the argument between Voltaire and David Goodhart.

There seem to be some parallels in the underlying trends in social capital in Britain and America. The most sweeping study in the United States suggests a story of near remorseless decline (Putnam, 2000) in most forms of social capital. One influential analysis suggested a somewhat more mixed picture in Britain, concluding that although trust had declined, participation had not (Hall, 1999). But more recent studies suggest Britain's total social capital has declined over the years, albeit in an economically skewed manner, with the biggest declines among the poor (Li et al., 2003; Grenier and Wright, 2006).

So, there do seem to be important similarities. But even if there are some transatlantic differences in the starting point for social capital, these could have arisen for any number of reasons. Such differences would not rule out the possibility that growing diversity affects community life in the same way in both countries. This chapter aims to discover whether or not this is in fact the case.

No one has done such a tightly focused British-American comparison before. But in different countries around the world, various studies have stepped on to similar ground before. One study across 44 different countries (Anderson and Paskeviciute, 2006) finds that diversity does damage trust, but establishes no clear link with participation. That is consistent with the official findings in Britain (Pennant, 2005), which also suggest that diversity tends to cut trust.

True, not all the studies point in the same direction. One in Britain (Laurence and Heath, 2008) reaches an apparently contradictory conclusion, suggesting that once allowance is made for a range of factors, including deprivation, diversity may actually increase community cohesion. But one of the factors that paper controls for is trust, which – at least on our definition – is a component of social capital. Reduced trust may also be the channel through which diversity undermines community participation, a channel closed off by controlling the results for the effects of trust. So even this apparently more sanguine analysis does not dispel the gloomy general picture.

While many of these studies make the point that social and economic deprivation affect social capital more adversely than diversity, it is true to say that – with trust at least – the evidence seems to run with the pessimists, those who predict contact will lead to conflict. The same is true with the initial findings for the US reported in the first half of Putnam (2007). Indeed, this paper finds a negative link not just with trust, but on other indicators of social capital too. However, by drilling down into exactly what *type* of trust is diminished, the Putnam (2007) study transcends the old conflict–contact debate. Doing so reveals that living in a mixed neighbourhood *does not* affect specifically interracial mistrust. Rather, diversity seems to damage, for instance, white-on-white interpersonal trust just as much as white-on-black trust. People do not retreat 'to their own' in order to take on rival races, it seems, but rather they respond to diversity by withdrawing from the community as a whole. So it is not a case of *conflict* at all, but rather of *constricting* one's social engagement overall in response to difference. In the paper's phrase, when faced with diversity, people tend to 'hunker down' – withdrawing into themselves in much the same way that a nervous turtle might withdraw into its shell.

English apples and American pears

We have plenty of information about communal life in both the UK and America. For the US there is the 2000 Social Capital Community Benchmark Study, which surveyed 30,000 respondents in 41 different locations, and asked them about trust in their neighbourhood, club membership and plenty more besides. On the British side, the 2005 Citizenship Survey of England and Wales asked questions covering the same sort of ground to nearly 10,000 people, as well as a booster sample of over 4,000 people from ethnic minorities.[48] Thanks to

---

[48] Putnam (2007) informs the construction of the US data set, and gives details on how this was done. For more details on the British data see the official documentation: www.communities.gov.uk/documents/communities/pdf/452581.pdf

special arrangements, we also have information about the characteristics of the locality in which each respondent lives – allowing us to explore the link between the communal life of each individual and the characteristics of the neighbourhood in which they live. These characteristics are obtained from official sources, such as the census, and crucially they include ethnic diversity.

The potential sticking point in comparing the relationship between diversity and communal life across the two countries, however, is that the exact indicators are not the same. In England and Wales, for example, respondents were asked about their 'unpaid activities' whereas Americans were asked, among other things, about whether they were an 'officer in a club'. While English respondents were asked whether others in their neighbourhood could be relied on to solve social problems, Americans were asked to rate their community. The danger, then, is of comparing apples with pears. To minimise this risk, we wove all the available data in both countries into two overall measures that capture the two main aspects of social capital – community-mindedness and community participation. Box 5.1 explains how this was done, while Table 5.1 (a and b) list the indicators that fit into each of these metrics.

Table 5.1a Questions used in our community-mindedness measure

England and Wales	America
How likely are local people to work together to solve a local community problem?	Rating of local community as a good place to live
Do people in the community pull together?	Do people in your neighbourhood give you a sense of community?
Do people in the neighbourhood share the same values?	How much can you trust people in your neighbourhood?
Is this a close-knit neighbourhood?	
Can people in your neighbourhood be trusted?	
Strength of belonging to neighbourhood	
How far are locals willing to help their neighbours?	

Table 5.1b Questions used in our community participation measure

England and Wales	America
Member of a civic group, such as a regeneration or public services board?	Worked on a community project in the last 12 months?
Have you taken part in a consultation about local services or local problems?	Serve as an officer or on a committee of a local club or organisation?
Help other people more than once a month?	Participate in various groups, including school support, sporting and unions?
Participate in various groups, including recreation clubs, religious groups and unions?	

Box 5.1 Measuring social capital

Just like intelligence, social capital cannot be seen directly. To gauge it, we borrow from psychometrics, where Item Response Theory has developed to 'get at' important things, such as intelligence, that cannot be directly observed by using something that can be observed, such as answers on an exam paper. In particular, we want to get at two different underlying aspects of social capital – community-mindedness and community participation – on the basis of different survey questions on the two sides of the Atlantic.

We have all sorts of relevant pointers – for example, in the case of community participation, group activity and volunteering. But how should we decide exactly how useful each of them is in gauging an individual's overall social capital? Just as having more intelligence makes it more likely a student will get any given exam question right, being more community-minded makes it more likely that an individual will volunteer, be trusting or indeed join a bridge club. The most telling exam questions – those which best discriminate between smart and dull students – are the best gauge of underlying intelligence, and therefore also the best predictor of how well a student will answer most other questions. Likewise, doing voluntary work is likely to be a good indicator of social capital if it is also a good predictor of participating in the community in other ways.

Thus, borrowing from IRT, our first step is to explore the strength of the statistical link between the various indicators in turn. On the basis of information about the strength of such links, we assign a weight to each indicator. That weight determines how important each indicator is in the final calculation of our two social capital measures, community-mindedness and participation.[49]

---

[49]The explanation here of the relationship between the individual indicators and the latent social capital variables is somewhat simplified. A fuller account of the method, the results obtained and their robustness is available in Fieldhouse and Cutts (2009).

Diversity and the social capital of white people

By concentrating on these two underlying measures of community-mindedness and community participation, we have sidestepped awkward differences in the detailed wording of questions between the American and the British study, making comparison easier. Next, we measure the ethnic mix of each respondent's neighbourhood by calculating an 'index of diversity' for their immediate neighbourhood using census data.[50] As an example of the crude relationship between the two, Figure 5.1 shows the average score on our community-mindedness index for white Britons who live in neighbourhoods at different points on the diversity scale.

Figure 5.1 Lost in the mix? Community-mindedness scores are lower for white Britons living in more diverse neighbourhoods

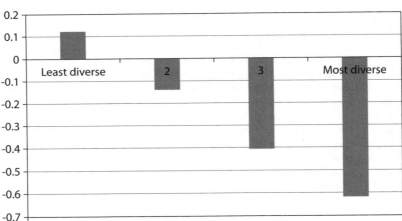

Notes: The community-mindedness scores shown are standardised, such that the whole-population mean is zero. Communities are grouped into four brackets, from the least diverse to the most diverse, depending on a fragmentation index. The various brackets are defined in terms of the level of that index rather than calibrated to contain an equal number of communities, and so contain differing numbers of communities and differing numbers of individuals.

[50]The index is the standard fragmentation index. In the UK the neighbourhood is fixed by the census's Middle Layer Super Output Area, which typically contains around 7,000 people. The US neighbourhoods are defined by (similarly sized) census tracts. See Fieldhouse and Cutts (2009) for more details.

The chart shows that white individuals in more diverse places in England and Wales do indeed seem to be less community-minded than those who live in more homogeneous areas. But this could, of course, be because of something other than the ethnic make-up of the neighbourhood. Mixed neighbourhoods are frequently poorer, for example, and they may also be more urban; the respondents who live in these areas may also be younger on average.

To unpick all of this, we run statistical tests ('regressions') which allow us to estimate the strength of the link between the thing we are interested in (social capital) and the factor we are most interested in (diversity) while holding other factors constant. The individual attributes we 'control for' include sex, educational attainment, class, income and the length of time a particular person has lived in their neighbourhood.[51] The neighbourhood characteristics we control for include indicators of poverty, inequality, crime and population turnover (or churn) within the neighbourhood.[52] Figures 5.2a and 5.2b show the strength of the link between diversity and our two measures of social capital, both before and after controlling for these factors, in Britain and America. The strength of the link is measured by the 'standardised coefficient'.

Figure 5.2a shows the impact on community-mindedness, and it does seem to show a clear link. The coefficients are generally negative, as they represent the negative relationship between diversity and social capital. (We multiply them by -1 in order to make them easier to present.) The raw results of -0.16 for England and Wales and -0.20 for the US imply a negative relationship between diversity and social capital, although a somewhat less negative one in Britain than in the US. We will come back to the question of just how big these effects really are, but we can immediately run tests that do enable us to deem this raw result statistically significant in both countries

---

[51]See Fieldhouse and Cutts (2009) for more details of controls used.

[52]Due to differences in data availability the measures are sometimes different in the two countries. In particular, inequality is assessed using a measure of income dispersion in the US, and poverty is also calculated on an income basis. The UK census does not ask about family income, and so inequality is assessed by a measure of the diversity of social class within an area, while poverty is gauged on the basis of factors including the receipt of means-tested benefits. See Fieldhouse and Cutts (2009) for more details.

Figure 5.2a Negative impact of diversity on community-mindedness for whites in Britain and the US

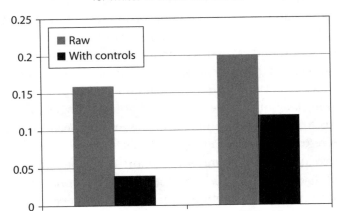

Figure 5.2b Minimal impact of diversity on community participation of whites in Britain, but some effect in the US

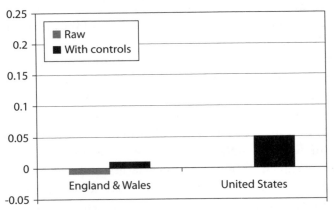

Notes: measured by standardised regression coefficients, multiplied by -1 to simplify the presentation. The 'Raw' bar for the US is not visible, because the standard coefficient in this case is zero.

– that is, we can be 95 per cent confident it is not the product of any chance error in our data.

The apparent relationship, however, could still be the result of something other than diversity – the lack of education among citizens in the ghettos, for instance, or the crime rates in such areas. So, next we add in a range of controls as described above, both for individual and for neighbourhood characteristics. This reduces the power of the link between diversity and community-mindedness by three-quarters in Britain (reducing the coefficient from -0.16 to -0.04) and by two-fifths in the US (reducing it from -0.20 to -0.12).

Thus most of the apparently adverse effect of diversity on community-mindedness for whites in Britain, which we saw displayed in Figure 5.1, was indeed the product of other factors – including poverty and crime in the area. The test of statistical significance, however, again suggests that the link remains too powerful in both countries to be explained away by any quirk in our data. Even after allowing for just about every available indicator that might have a bearing on trust within a community, diversity still seems to be having a negative effect on those attitudes that support community living, and especially so in America.

If we look instead at how community participation is affected by diversity, the story is different. As Figure 5.2b shows the link between diversity and this measure is almost non-existent in Britain – whether or not controls are included. Indeed, if we run the tests for statistical significance, they confirm that in Britain there is no meaningful link. In America, by contrast, once the characteristics of more diverse neighbourhoods are taken into account by adding controls, diversity does emerge as having a meaningful and negative effect, albeit one that is somewhat smaller than that for community-mindedness.

Overall, our analysis suggests that diversity does have some negative consequences for social capital in both Britain and America, and particularly so in the United States. In both countries, however, participation is less sensitive to diversity than community-mindedness. If, as David Goodhart suggests, diversity damages social solidarity, our results suggest it does so chiefly by damaging attitudes, such as trust, rather than by discouraging sociable behaviour.

Appreciable, but not all-important: the diversity effect in perspective

Even if the negative link between diversity and community-mindedness is real, the extent to which it is worth worrying about depends upon its power – just how much of an impact will an increase in neighbourhood diversity really have on levels of trust? The standardised coefficients do not lend themselves to ready interpretation, but we can go back to the data and calculate an example for the US, the country where our charts have suggested the diversity effect is most pronounced, in order to gauge just how important it is.

For the average white American, we can calculate that moving from the least diverse to the most diverse neighbourhood in the American data shifts the typical community-mindedness score from 0.06 to -0.04.[53] This score is another complex statistical construct, but it is one that we can now relate back to the three survey questions which we used to measure community-mindedness in the first place – whether or not one feels a sense of community, whether or not one feels the neighbourhood is a good place to live, and whether or not the respondent feels others in their area can be trusted. Roughly speaking, we calculate that – when all else is equal – the shift from the least diverse to the most diverse neighbourhood would be associated with around an extra 10 per cent of people giving a negative answer to one of these three questions. Recall that we have moved from one end of the diversity spectrum to the other extreme, and this effect – one in ten people registering as appreciably less community-minded on one of three indicators – does not seem particularly large. The equivalent impact in the UK would be somewhat less marked.

Another way to get some perspective on the effect is to compare it with the strain put on social capital by other factors. When we 'control for' characteristics other than diversity in the regression analysis, each of these other factors gets a coefficient of its own. Figure 5.3 compares the size of the standardised coefficients for diversity with those for other factors that operate at the neighbourhood level. It shows that in Britain, neighbourhood poverty does far more damage to community-mindedness than does diversity: its effect is nearly three times bigger. In America, deprivation within a neighbourhood also seems to be a somewhat more important driver of hunkering down than does diversity. This time, however, the difference

---

[53]The community-mindedness score is a standardised normal variable with a mean of zero and a standard deviation of one. See Fieldhouse and Cutts (2009) for more details on how the shift in its score is calculated from the regression coefficients.

Figure 5.3 The negative effect of diversity on community-mindedness compared to other neighbourhood factors, whites in Britain and the US

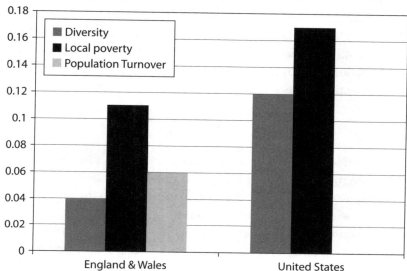

Notes: Figures are standardised coefficients. To simplify presentation all coefficients have been multiplied by -1. Somewhat different measures of poverty are shown for Britain and the US. In the US, local poverty rates are based on comparing census income data to a local poverty line. In the British census there is no income question, so neighbourhood poverty is measured using a deprivation index that is based on factors such as the number of families in the areas receiving means-tested benefits. Population turnover is measured as the proportion of residents in an area to have moved in recently.

is much less stark – the coefficients of 0.12 for diversity and 0.17 for poverty are at least in neighbouring ballparks.

The churning of the population is another thing that might be expected to undermine social capital. If, instead of settling down in a neighbourhood, families are forever moving in and out, then – counter to the old song from the soap – good neighbours will not become good friends. In Britain, the importance of turnover to community-mindedness turns out to be rather more marked than that of diversity. (The American figure is not shown on the chart as our statistical tests suggest this factor does not meaningfully affect the community-mindedness score.)

To recap, diversity does seem to adversely affect community-mindedness, but it is only one of several relevant factors. In England

and Wales, poverty corrodes the attitudes of sociability far more gravely and population churn is also somewhat more important than diversity. In America, the diversity effect is more pronounced, but even there poverty is somewhat more important. And when the focus shifts from the attitudes that support community living to actual community participation, the diversity effect is reduced in America and it disappears entirely in Britain.

Hunkering down among minorities

Is the turtle-style response to diversity principally a phenomenon of the white majority or does it apply to minorities too? In the rest of this chapter, we pursue this question in greater depth than it has been pursued before. As well as being interesting in its own right, the reaction of minorities in isolation will provide us with the means to delve into the question of exactly *how* diversity affects social capital.

There are at least two reasons to suspect that minorities might respond differently to diversity from the white majority. First of all, diversity in itself may provide a benefit to minorities that it does not offer to whites – namely, it may make them stand out less, which may in turn help them to *build bridges* to others in the community. Consider the first African family to move on to an estate. If everyone else on the estate is white there is perhaps more of a risk they will be treated as an odd one out than if the neighbourhood already contained a number of Chinese and Indian people.

Even if this turns out not to be true, there is a second reason why the response might be different. Namely, for members of minorities, more diverse areas may tend to provide a chance to live alongside more people from one's own particular ethnic group. Vast swaths of both the US and UK remain the near-exclusive preserve of whites and if, say, an Indian family moves from one such district to a cosmopolitan borough, then they are much more likely to come into contact with other Indians.[54] This is especially true in the UK, where – as Chapter 3 showed – very few minorities live in (low diversity)

---

[54] This effect for minorities is the opposite of that for whites – a white person moving to a more diverse area will become relatively less likely to meet other whites.

ghettos. If people really do find it easier to *bond* with others of their own ethnic group, then diversity might appear to provide particular benefits to minority groups.

As we examine the impact of diversity upon the community life of minorities, the distinctive potential effects on *bonding* (within-group) and *bridging* (between-group) social capital should be borne in mind. Either of these potentially distinctive effects could result in diversity impacting on ethnic minorities in different ways from on the white majority.

First of all, let us examine the crude relationship between neighbourhood diversity and social capital for minority individuals, before we take into account poverty or anything else. As in Figure 5.1 for whites, we will focus on community-mindedness in England and Wales as an example. Figure 5.4 shows that among minorities, as among whites, there is a negative relationship between diversity and social

Figure 5.4 Community-mindedness scores for white and minority Britons in neighbourhoods with different levels of diversity

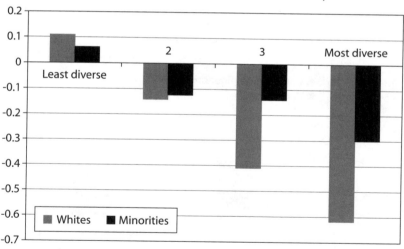

Notes: Communities are grouped into four brackets, from the least diverse to the most diverse, depending on a fragmentation index. The various brackets are defined in terms of the level of that index rather than calibrated to contain an equal number of communities, and so contain differing numbers of communities and differing numbers of individuals. The community-mindedness scores shown are standardised, such that the whole-population mean is zero.

capital. But the relationship is markedly less steep this time. In particular, the community-mindedness score of minority ethnic individuals
is less negative than it is for whites in the same sort of neighbourhoods.
So this chart hints that diversity might indeed affect minorities in
different ways.

Our initial statistical tests, however, suggest there is still a negative relationship between diversity and community-mindedness among
ethnic minorities, and rules out the possibility that it is down to chance.
Indeed, unlike among whites, for whom the effect was chiefly felt on
community-mindedness, among minorities there is also a significant negative link between diversity and participation.[55] Once again,
however, this apparent relationship may be nothing more than a
reflection of the non-racial characteristics of diverse areas, and the
people who live in them. The interesting question is what happens
when we control for these, a question answered in Figure 5.5.

The first thing to notice is the scale of the effects – for community-
mindedness they are small, so small in fact that detailed tests suggest there is not a statistically significant relationship at all. Where,

Figure 5.5 Negative impact of diversity on social capital for non-whites in
Britain and the US, after controlling for individual and neighbourhood characteristics

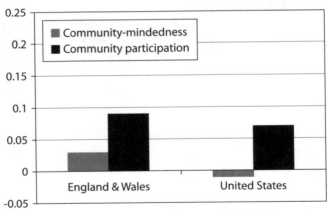

Note: Measured by standardised regression coefficients multiplied by -1.

[55] Full regression results – with and without controls – available in Fieldhouse and Cutts
(2009).

for whites, community-mindedness had a meaningful effect on social capital in both Britain and the US, it does so in neither country this time. Indeed, with community-mindedness for minorities in the US, to the extent there is a relationship at all, it is reversed – greater diversity is weakly associated with more positive attitudes. Intriguingly, the chart reports that diversity significantly reduces participation for minorities on both sides of the Atlantic, even though it had no effect on white Britons. This further encourages the notion that diversity impacts on minorities in different ways from whites.

At least for community-mindedness, then, greater diversity does not have the same adverse effect for minorities that it does for whites. The next question is whether this lesser overall effect can be explained by diversity having some distinctive benefit to the community life of ethnic minorities, which offsets the negative effect. Recall the *bridging* hypothesis (diversity saves minority ethnic individuals from standing out) and the *bonding* theory (in diverse areas, minorities more often live alongside others from their own ethnic group, and this makes them more community-minded): could either of these be having an effect?

The first step to testing the bonding hypothesis is to calculate an index of 'co-ethnic density' – that is a measure of the proportion of people from an individual's own particular ethnic minority who live in that individual's neighbourhood. In principle, co-ethnicity can be calculated for whites, too, but whites predominate so thoroughly across so much of both Britain and the US that the index for them is little more than a mirror image of diversity.[56] For ethnic minorities, however, the relationship is different. In England and Wales, greater diversity tends to go hand in hand with greater co-ethnicity for individuals from minorities because, as we saw in Chapter 3, most minority ethnic individuals live in places where they constitute a small proportion of the population.[57] In the US, though, while many members of minority groups are dispersed across white-dominated

---

[56]The correlation between diversity and co-ethnic density for whites (i.e. percentage white) is -0.96 in England and -0.86 in the US. And indeed, the effect on whites' social capital of greater co-ethnic density is more or less a mirror image of the effect of diversity. See Fieldhouse and Cutts (2009) for more detail on the results.

[57]The correlation coefficient is +0.46.

Figure 5.6 Positive effect of co-ethnic density on community-mindedness for British minorities, and on both community-mindedness and community participation for American minorities

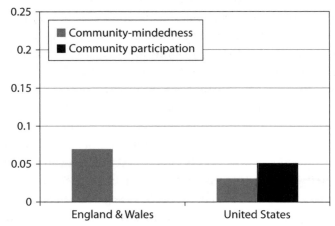

Notes: Measured by standardised regression coefficients. Unlike in other charts in this chapter, the coefficients are not multiplied by -1 because this chart is representing a positive rather than a negative association. Results are after controlling for individual and neighbourhood characteristics. The bar for the community participation of British minorities is not visible because the standard coefficient in this case is zero.

neighbourhoods, many others are clustered in ghettos, as Chapter 3 showed. As a result there is little link between diversity and co-ethnicity for minorities in the States, rendering the *bonding* theory less tenable as an explanation for the lesser impact of diversity on the community-mindedness of minorities.[58]

We can now assess the effect of this new co-ethnicity index on social capital, applying the same method and set of controls that we have used in analysing diversity. Figure 5.6 shows the results. In England and Wales, co-ethnicity has a significantly positive effect on community-mindedness, suggesting, perhaps, that for many British ethnic minorities, the debate about whether the country is 'sleepwalking into segregation' may be wide of the mark. All else being equal, the typical minority Briton will be more community-minded – that is more trusting, more comfortable in their community – the more people of their own minority are living nearby. In the United States,

[58]The correlation coefficient is -0.10.

by contrast, the chart shows only a small positive link, which turns out not to be statistically significant: the coefficient is so small its true value could well be zero. This transatlantic difference could well reflect the special nature of the African American ghetto, where – as we saw in Chapter 3 – very many residents wish they lived elsewhere. America's ghettos may provide minorities with a chance to live alongside their co-ethnics, but they do not encourage trust.

Again, however, the results for participation somewhat complicate the picture. The analysis suggests that community activity is supported by co-ethnic density for minorities in the US. Regardless of levels of trust in the neighbourhood, perhaps ethnic homogeneity somehow supports engagement with certain religious or other organisations.

The final question is how these co-ethnicity effects should colour interpretation of the impact of diversity. The tendency for co-ethnicity to support some forms of social capital lends support to our *bonding* theory – that diversity helps minority individuals build social capital by allowing them to live alongside more members of their own ethnic group. With this effect 'switched off', do ethnic minorities respond any differently to diversity? Figure 5.7 runs the experiment.

Figure 5.7 Negative effect of diversity on social capital for non-whites in Britain and the US allowing for co-ethnic density

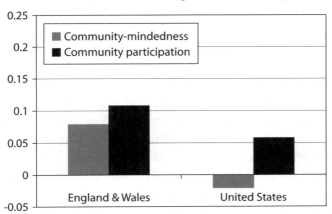

Notes: Measured by standardised regression coefficients. Coefficients multiplied by -1 to simplify the presentation. Results control for a full range of individual and neighbourhood characteristics, as well as for co-ethnic density.

The chart recalculates the effect of diversity after controlling not just for all the local and individual characteristics we have considered before, but also for co-ethnic density.

In England and Wales, at least, it suggests that – once the concentration of co-ethnics is allowed for – minorities are not so different from whites. Diversity now has a significantly adverse effect on community-mindedness. Its damaging effect stands in particular contrast to the insignificant relationship seen in Figure 5.5, before co-ethnicity was taken into account. Indeed, the adverse effect is now somewhat larger than was the effect for British whites. Contrary to the *bridging* hypothesis, diversity of itself does not seem to offer minorities any special benefit. Once co-ethnicity is allowed for, diversity causes English minorities to hunker down in much the same way as whites. In the context of England and Wales, the *bonding* hypothesis – the theory that people feel more comfortable around others of their own particular race – provides a feasible explanation for why diversity *appears* to affect minorities and whites in different ways.

Thus for British minorities, a beneficial by-product of living in a diverse neighbourhood may be the chance to 'to be with one's own'. But once the effect of living alongside others from one's own particular race is allowed for, diversity still imposes a strain – a strain that seems to flow from the discomfort that some experience in dealing with people from a variety of races. It is impossible to run the same experiment for whites, because co-ethnicity and (a lack of) diversity are too closely entwined for it to be statistically possible to unpick the two in a meaningful way. But it is hard to see why this conclusion would not read across to British whites as well.

In the United States, by contrast, the *bonding* theory was never as plausible an explanation for the lack of a clear link between diversity and community-mindedness among ethnic minorities. That is because – thanks to the existence of more ethnic ghettos and enclaves – greater diversity is not associated with greater co-ethnic density for minorities in the US in the way that it is for minorities in England. And indeed, the American results here are barely distinguishable from what they were before co-ethnicity was considered. The effect of diversity on community-mindedness is still not statistically significant, and the previous slight tendency for diversity to *increase* community-mindedness is now somewhat more marked. That makes for quite a contrast with whites, and thus lends tentative support to the *bridging* hypothesis – suggesting that for American minorities the difficulties of being 'an odd one out' in a homogeneous area may be sufficient to offset the general tendency of diversity to encourage hunkering down.

Conclusions

Diversity could, and no doubt does, affect community life through all sorts of channels – some good and some bad. It may foster beneficial contact between ethnicities, it may bring out an instinctive fear of difference in some individuals and it may threaten the bond of 'common values and assumptions' that David Goodhart talked about in the quote at the top of this chapter. This chapter has not sought to evaluate separately the contribution of the various potential channels, all of which might be important. Rather, it has sought to measure their *combined* effect – which *could* be to strengthen or weaken community life.

The big picture, in line with Putnam (2007), is that – in the context of contemporary Britain and America – the overall effect tends to be to strain community-mindedness. The conclusion is reinforced because, among whites at least, it is found to operate in very similar ways on the two sides of the Atlantic, albeit more powerfully in the USA.

While significant, however, the strain from diversity is not as great as that which arises from neighbourhood poverty – being far less marked in Britain, and somewhat smaller in America. Among white Americans diversity reduces participation, too, but the same is not true in Britain. The fact diversity does not deter community involvement in England and Wales encourages particular optimism on the question of whether – over time – diversity might cease to be a strain in the UK. The lessons of American history, however, provide grounds for broader optimism on both sides of the Atlantic.

To the extent that today's Britons and Americans would rather 'live with their own' and avoid racial 'others', this is largely a product of a particular and potentially impermanent racial cleavage in society.

Two generations ago, in America at least, religious denominations formed another such dividing line – reflected in who married whom, and who prayed with whom – but faith does not form such a divide today. Where previous waves of immigration caused divisions in their day, the gradual Americanisation of St Patrick's Day, pizza and 'Jewish' humour all demonstrate how over time it is possible to build a more capacious sense of 'we'. The remarkable integration of the US army meanwhile – which was still formally segregated in the Second World War and still riven with racial tension in Vietnam, but where today interracial friendships are more likely than in America as a whole – provides another heartening reminder of how inter-ethnic divisions can heal and fade over time.[59]

We will return to some of this in the Conclusion, and we will also find more cause for hope in Chapter 7. For now, however, the strain diversity imposes is real, and by isolating the effect on ethnic minorities this chapter has shed new light on its nature. At first blush, in neither Britain nor America does diversity reduce community-mindedness for minorities in the way that it does for whites. But when we shift our focus to the effect of living near one's co-ethnics the picture in the two countries changes in different ways. In the US, home of the African American ghetto described in Chapter 3, the effect on minorities of living with 'their own kind' is – if anything – negative. For (relatively diffuse) British minority ethnic individuals, however, living alongside more of their co-ethnics turns out to have a positive effect. The upshot is that the development of ethnic enclaves in the UK may be helping to foster the sort of attitudes that support community.

Once the positive co-ethnicity effect is stripped out, however, British minorities respond to diversity by hunkering down, in much the same way as whites. This is one sign that the strains diversity imposes do not just reflect a desire 'to live among one's own' but also a discomfort with encountering difference. The next chapter explores what happens when voices in the media and politics seek to exploit that emotion.

[59]This argument is taken from Putnam (2007), where it is made more expansively.

6

Distorting mirrors: media framing and political debate

The Conservative slogan in Britain's 2005 election – 'Are you thinking what we're thinking?' – signalled a cut-the-crap approach and
folksy intimacy with the electorate, the strapline equivalent, perhaps,
of Vice-Presidential hopeful Sarah Palin's famous wink during
America's 2008 campaign. But the Tory twist was to add a second
slogan: 'it's not racist to talk about immigration'. Together, these
messages winked at voters that the Conservatives were fed up with
taboos that stifled the airing of popular resentment. The second
slogan also pulled off the ingenious trick of linking race and migration in the electorate's mind at the same time as insisting they were
separate. Veiled references to race have, of course, been made before,
especially in American Republican campaigns on crime and welfare
between the late 1960s and the mid-1990s. This time, however, the
reference and the veil were one and the same – the slogan brazenly
proclaimed its own innocence.

Controversy sells almost as well as sex, and so this none-too-subtle
assault on supposed political correctness around immigration loomed
large in press reporting during the campaign. Having established in
the last chapter that discomfort with diversity is real, we now turn
to consider what happens when prominent voices give it an airing,
as happened during the 2005 British campaign.

Reporting, resentment and reality

The media deals in mood music as well as relaying the facts – and
indeed, when it comes to immigration the facts are sometimes treated
with outright contempt. One apocryphal headline from the UK's most

widely read newspaper in 2003 is a telling reminder that, even if overt racism is nowadays taboo, freewheeling fictions are still used to slander immigrants. 'Swan Bake', the *Sun* splashed across its front page, as it asserted that 'callous asylum seekers' were illegally killing and eating a bird, which is not only popular but, by English custom, owned by the Queen. Subsequently a clarification, buried away on page 41, admitted that the link with asylum seekers was pure conjecture, and indeed that no one at all had been arrested in connection with the rumoured swan culling.

There are many such anecdotes, of course. But we can also demonstrate the systematic mismatch between objective reality and press interest in immigration rather more methodically, using some recent American data. Figure 6.1 shows the spike of concern about immigration in the US press in 2006, and reveals that this was not immediately preceded by a surge in immigration, and indeed that net immigration to America had been somewhat higher in previous years.

Like media coverage, public concern with immigration also seems disconnected from the number of newcomers coming into the country. In truth, American immigration had peaked around 1997 and remained high for a few years after that before declining somewhat. At a time when immigration remained close to its peak, in February 2001, the Pew survey asked 785 Americans an open-ended question about the most pressing problems facing their communities, and not a single one named immigration. Compare that with another Pew survey in 2006 – by which time immigration was slightly lower, but which came after congressional action and pro-immigrant marches had put immigration on the agenda – when fully 19 per cent of non-Hispanic respondents named immigration as 'a very big problem in my local community'.[60] Gallup polling from the same period underlines that public opinion is far too volatile to be explained by demographics alone: in January 2006, just 3 per cent of Americans

---

[60]The wording of this question was different. But even with an open-ended question more like that asked in 2001, 19 of the 864 individuals (2.2 per cent) named immigration as the biggest single issue for their community. The percentage is small but 19 individuals is still an appreciable increase from the zero recorded in the 2001 survey.

Figure 6.1 The surge of US media interest in 2006 was actually preceded by falling rates of immigration into America

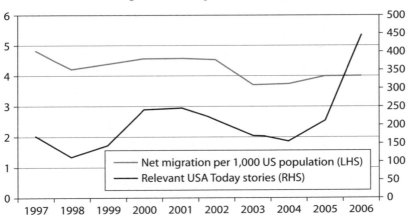

Source: Immigration figures from the Organization for Economic Cooperation and Development's Factbook; *USA Today* report figures are annual averages, collated in Hopkins (2009).
Note: LHS = left-hand side axis; RHS = right-hand side axis.

named immigration as the nation's most important problem, but that had spiked to 19 per cent a mere three months later.[61]

While the ebbs and flows of public anxieties bear little relation to actual migration flows then, they frequently *do* correspond to the rhetorical pitch in the national debate. There was, for instance, a short-lived spike in the number of column inches being churned out on immigration after the 9/11 terror attacks; it was too brief to be visible in the annual series on *USA Today's* coverage in Figure 6.1 but can be discerned in the underlying data. Opinion polling from the same time suggests that this spike was mirrored in rising public concern.[62] Likewise in modern Britain, race and migration have periodically been brought to the forefront of both the news agenda and public concern by riots, terrorist attacks and international events (Solomos, 1993). The unanswered question, though, is which way the causality flows. Do reporters and politicians merely reflect popular discomfort, or do they instead work to inflame it? Precisely because

[61]These results come from Gallup's monthly telephone surveys.
[62]See Hopkins (2007) for more detail.

public anxiety and press interest often move so closely together, this is not an easy question to settle.

Pointing the finger at cynical politicians and journalists is easy enough to do, and persuasive academic work has put the charge with subtlety. People perceive countless nuggets of information in their everyday lives – from the price of milk to traffic congestion to the appearance of Bengali translations of local council leaflets – any of which they could interpret as telling them something useful about society. Many of them *could* be deemed to have political significance, but most of us have little time for politics and so we take our lead from the news in deciding which issues to regard this way (Iyengar and Kinder, 1987). As well as serving as a *filter*, news reports and the political rhetoric they convey are a *conversation starter*. If an issue such as immigration gets a good deal of press attention then individuals will assume 'common knowledge'[63] of it on the part of others they encounter, and thus regard it as a suitable subject to raise over the garden fence or in the local pub. And the more something is talked about, the more aware of it people become – if, for instance, you have heard a friend observe that the local shop has started selling beer marketed at Poles, you become more likely to notice it yourself.

But whatever the theory, it is hard to prove conclusively that journalists trying to sell papers and politicians trying to win votes are doing anything more than passively responding to what the public thinks. After all, we have seen both that Britain and America have become incomparably more diverse than they used to be over the last several decades and that this diversity can take a toll on attitudes such as trust. Even if the rate of immigration at any one moment does not correspond with public anxiety about it, maybe this underlying discomfort flares up from time to time without any help from politicians – whether in response to events such as 9/11 or spontaneously. If so, then it could still be that politicians do not so much stoke public fears about immigration as give expression to them.

The best way to settle this argument is to ask the same people the same questions about immigration immediately before and immediately

---

[63]See Chwe (2001).

after a sudden turning-up of the political temperature. Happily, the British Election Survey of 2005 did just that, conducting face-to-face interviews with 2,959 respondents – immediately before and then immediately after the campaign.[64] Figure 6.2a shows how the two waves of BES interviews were conducted either side of a great surge of media interest in the immigration issue.

A matter of mere weeks separates many of the interviews, and besides the sudden frenzy of political interest sparked by the 'are you thinking what we're thinking' campaign, it is hard to see what else could have so increased the salience of the coverage of immigration in the media in such a short space of time. Any deep current of hostility to immigrants that started with the public themselves, one might have thought, would have been likely to build up much more slowly. And yet public opinion certainly changed. As Figure 6.2b shows, whereas just 12.9 per cent of respondents ranked immigration or asylum as their top issue before the campaign, 21.4 per cent did so afterwards – *a proportional increase of two-thirds*.

That seems like an extraordinary change, but just how robust is this finding – could it be a consequence of the particular measure of voter anxiety that we are using? Now, it is true that during an election campaign the public's concern with all manner of issues is likely to increase, as these are drawn to their attention. But remember that we are here considering what voters tell pollsters they regard as the *single most important* issue, so this should be a gauge of relative, not absolute, voter concern – a test of how concerned people are about immigration *relative* to other issues. Still, it might be objected that after the campaign the electorate will be better informed, and so less likely to say they don't know or don't care about what the most important issue is, something that would cause the scores for all issues to increase. And indeed, a growing proportion of voters came to identify most of the big issues as being the single top priority over the course of the campaign. Look at a selection of the other big

---

[64]There were 3,589 initial interviews and 2,959 individuals who were successfully re-interviewed. But our figures and analysis are concentrated on the sub-sample of 2,386 white Britons within the latter. The overwhelming majority of the pre-election interviews took place before the announcement of the election on 11 April. The vast majority of the post-election interviews were completed within two months after the election on 5 May.

Figure 6.2a Two waves of polling divided by a surge of press interest in immigration, the British Election Survey 2005

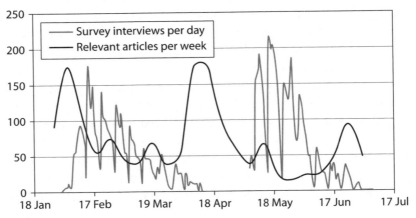

Figure 6.2b The surge of press interest is followed by a surge in public anxiety about immigration

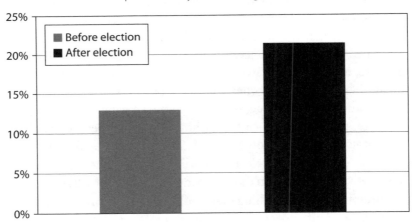

Notes: Election day was 5 May 2005. 'Relevant articles' in 6.2a is the number of news stories per week mentioning 'race', 'immigration', 'immigrants', or 'asylum' in a sample of roughly 100 British newspapers available through Lexis-Nexis. 'Interviews' in 6.2a is simply the number of pre- and post-election BES interviews carried out per day. Figure 6.2b records the weighted proportion of respondents citing 'immigration' or 'asylum' as the biggest problem facing the country.

issues, however, and it becomes clear that both the absolute and the proportional rise for immigration were quite exceptionally large.[65] The upshot is that the election made a difference to concern about immigration, and that it made more of a difference than it did for other issues.

At elections, as at no other time, politicians are guaranteed air-time and so should have the chance to make the political weather. There is every reason to think that the Conservatives were pro-active about turning migration into what was, in the verdict of Britain's most seasoned election-watchers, a dominant issue of the campaign (Kavanagh and Butler, 2005). For one thing, they hired in the former adviser to the Australian Prime Minister John Howard, Lynton Crosby. In 2001 Howard had pulled off a surprise election victory after turning away a Norwegian ship carrying asylum seekers by sending Australian forces on board. Ever since then, whether fairly or not, Crosby had been associated with so-called 'dog whistle' campaigning – which conveys unpleasant messages that only some voters can pick up on. Even before Crosby's arrival, Michael Howard had reportedly identified migration as a campaign theme.[66]

So, it seems, the Conservative party tried to make migration an issue, and the British Election Study suggests they succeeded – powerful evidence that words *can* have power over opinion. But political rhetoric does not develop in a vacuum, and nor does it always persuade. Next we turn to consider, on both sides of the Atlantic, when it has most power.

The local dimension: where words make a difference

The most notorious speech made on immigration by a senior British politician in recent decades was delivered by the Conservative Enoch

[65]Before the election, 14.6 per cent of the British panel respondents said the most important issue facing Britain was the National Health Service; after, it was 16.1 per cent, an increase of 1.5 per cent, or around one-tenth. For law and order, there was an increase of a third – from 8.9 per cent to 11.7 per cent; for education the rise was of about one-seventh, from 5.7 per cent to 6.6 per cent; for terrorism, by contrast, there was a decline, from 5.4 per cent to 2.0 per cent afterwards.

[66]'The Jeeves to Johnson's Bertie Wooster: The Man Who May Have Got Him Elected', *Guardian*, 2 May 2008.

Powell, in 1968. A somewhat other-worldly classical scholar, Powell proclaimed: 'Like the Roman, I seem to see "the River Tiber foaming with much blood"', wrongly predicting that continuing immigration would soon lead to British society tearing itself apart. His argument was laced with untruths, but one of Powell's lines does resonate with the so-called 'conflict theory' that cropped up in the previous chapter. 'Numbers are of the essence', he said, with the significance of the 'alien element' being 'profoundly different according to whether that element is 1 per cent or 10 per cent'.

Ever since V. O. Key's work on black and white Americans in the Deep South (Key, 1949), one stream of research has analysed ethnic relations at the local level in terms of competition for resources – whether political or material, whether control of the council or priority on the council house list. And *if* such competitions are important, then where immigrants are more numerous they will be perceived as more of a *threat*, because they will be better placed to challenge the indigenous for control. But this caricature of competition and threat seems a crude way of understanding how different populations – each of them made up of different individuals – interact with each other. The evidence that it captures reality is decidedly mixed – several studies have failed to find a 'threatened' response to Hispanics or immigrants in the US.[67] Besides, having just established that political and media debates – debates overwhelmingly framed at the national level – are important in shaping attitudes, we already know that there is much more to the perception of threat than local demographics.

We need a subtler theory, which encompasses both media framing *and* local demographics. Perhaps people can be troubled by the number of immigrants living locally, but to do that they must have a good idea of how many of them there are, something they frequently do not possess.[68] Press attention may encourage people first to notice nearby immigrants, and then to start to resent them. If so, rhetoric

---

[67]See, for example, Taylor (1998).

[68]A survey of 113 respondents conducted by Daniel J. Hopkins in February 2008 found that Americans' guesses about the share of immigrants in their ZIP code correlated at just 0.23 with the correct figure.

will translate into resentment most decisively in diverse neighbour-hoods – such neighbourhoods will not just harbour most anxiety about immigration, but will also see that anxiety *rise disproportionately* when the political heat turns up.

Using Pew Opinion Poll data, we can put this prediction to the test for America in 2006 – a time at which, as we have seen, concern about immigration had flared up. All sorts of factors might affect an individual's anxiety about immigration – for instance, their educa-tion or ideology; and these things might be different on average for those individuals who live in districts that have absorbed the most immigrants. So, as in previous chapters, we use regression analysis, a statistical technique that allows us to examine each factor in turn, while holding other things constant.[69] Specifically, we control for an individual's ideology, partisanship, family income, age, race, sex and education.[70]

As well as the factor we are most interested in – the number of immigrants living in the district – other characteristics of the neigh-bourhood could make a difference as well. For example, in more affluent areas people might feel less inclined to see immigrants as a threat. Thus – using census information – we also control for the neighbourhood's average income and the proportion of its residents who are college graduates and the proportion who are black.[71] Finally, recent *change* in the number of immigrants could be important – locals might resent or fear the effect of newcomers more than longer-established minorities. Using information from the 2006 American Community Survey we also control for how far each of our other area-level factors has changed between the 2000 census and 2006.

The most important results are displayed in Figure 6.3, expressed as the percentage point *change in the chance of the average person deem-ing immigration a 'very big' problem* when the named factor shifts from

---

[69]The dependent variable is a four-category question about how significant immigration is as a problem in the respondent's local community. An 'ordered probit' regression is appro-priate to model such ordered categorical variables, and that is what is used in this case.

[70]Ideology scores based on the question, 'in general, would you describe your political views as very conservative, conservative, moderate, liberal, or very liberal'. Partisanship indicates a seven-category partisan identification question.

[71]Income is measured by the log of the neighbourhood's median household income.

Figure 6.3 Selected drivers of concern with immigration, America 2006

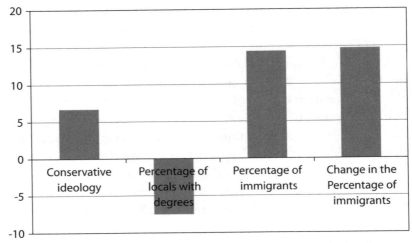

Note: Percentage point change in the likelihood of a respondent calling immigration a 'very big' problem when – holding all else equal – he or she shifts from a relatively low value (tenth percentile) to a relatively high value (90th percentile) for each of the indicators shown.

a low value to a high one.[72] By far the biggest effects shown on the chart are those for immigration. When the average person moves from a low- to a high-immigrant area, the chart shows that – all else being equal – they become nearly 15 percentage points more likely to regard immigration as a big problem. Move from a low- to a high-ranking area in terms of the *recent inflow* of newcomers and the effect is also 15 points. With such a move, the chance of regarding immigration as a 'very big' problem *more than doubles*, from 11 per cent to 26 per cent.

The relationship of public concern both to the local level of immigration and to the recent changes in its rate is statistically significant – that is, tests confirm a link too strong to be explained away by quirks in the survey.[73] That is not true of most of the other

[72]What counts as a 'low' and a 'high' value is fixed in relative terms. For each factor, all values are ranked in order – from highest to lowest – and the low value is taken as that which is one-tenth of the way up from the bottom of the table, while high value is that found a tenth of the way down from the top.

[73]See Hopkins (2009) for the confidence intervals.

factors we investigated, which have no meaningful relationship with public anxiety at all.[74] There are exceptions. As the chart shows, the number of college graduates in one's neighourhood does work to reduce concern, as does an increase in family income (which is not shown on the chart). Likewise, being at the conservative end of the ideological spectrum works instead to increase it. All of these effects are small, however, when set against the effect of immigration itself.

At first blush this might seem to suggest that demographics are all-powerful. How does our analysis relate back to the media or national politics? Recall that as recently as 2001 not a single American told the Pew poll that they regarded immigration as the top problem facing their community, but that this situation had changed significantly by 2006, by which time nearly a fifth of respondents rated immigration as 'a very big problem in my local community'. It therefore makes sense to assume that *virtually all* of the concern registered in our 2006 survey is an effect of a *change* in the level of anxiety – an emergence of anxiety associated with that surge in press interest in 2006, which was captured in Figure 6.1. The implication of Figure 6.3 is thus that media framing does indeed have most influence in those localities where immigration is making the biggest demographic impact.

With the British election of 2005 we can run a similar analysis[75] that focuses on the role of political debate with even greater precision. That is because we have information about the same individuals both before and after the election campaign – a campaign that we have already seen *did* change public opinion. Again, we will explore what drives people to be seriously concerned about immigration – this time, they are counted as such if they name either 'asylum' or 'immigration' as the most important issue facing the country. Again, we want to take account of a whole host of factors. We control for sex, age and income at the personal level, as well as a crude indicator of social class (whether or not the respondent is an unskilled worker) and party

---

[74]See Hopkins (2009) for more detail on the results.

[75]This time, the dependent variable is binary, so the regression model is a logistic regression, but the results are interpreted in the same way.

Figure 6.4 Percentage point change in power of selected drivers of concern with immigration, before and after Britain's 2005 election

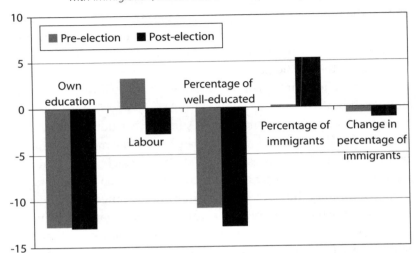

Note: Percentage point change in the likelihood of a respondent calling immigration a 'very big' problem when – holding all else equal – he or she shifts from a relatively low value (tenth percentile) to a relatively high value (90th percentile) for each of the indicators shown. For yes/no variables such as 'is Labour supporter', the shift will typically be from 'no' to 'yes'.

identification. At the neighbourhood level we factor in the proportion of the population in the highest social class, the proportion with higher qualifications[76] and population density. Finally, of course, we include a measure for the number of immigrants (the percentage born abroad) as well as *change* in migration (the number of immigrants arriving in the last year).

Figure 6.4 for the UK can be read in exactly the same way as Figure 6.3 for the US – it shows how the likelihood of harbouring serious concerns about immigration changes when an otherwise-average individual shifts from a low- to a high-rating for each of our factors in turn (per cent of immigrants in neighbourhood, level of education of neighbours, etc.). The only difference is that this time there are two results for each factor – one for before and one for after the election.

---

[76] Defined as Level 4 or 5 qualifications.

The striking thing about the pre-election results is that neither the number of immigrants nor the recent change in their number seems to have much impact at all. Moving to a more educated neighbourhood does affect the level of concern. But moving to a neighbourhood where there are more immigrants seems to make no real difference at all – the estimated effect is virtually zero, for both the level of immigration and the change in its rate. Statistical tests confirm that neither has any significant link with public anxiety before the election campaign.[77]

These pre-election results underline that *crude* threat theories are wide of the mark – living near numerous immigrants does not automatically trigger concern. But it does not follow that there is nothing at all in threat theory. Indeed, the post-election results strongly suggest that a heightening of the political rhetoric can switch the threat effect on. After the campaign and associated press furore, moving from a low- to a high-migrant area typically increases the chance of being seriously concerned about immigration by 6.3 percentage points. When only one in five respondents overall (21.4 per cent) harbour such concerns, this is a substantial effect. It is also statistically meaningful, being both significantly positive and significantly different from the pre-election result.[78]

Even after the election, however, the chart also shows that several other factors bear a closer connection with public anxiety than the rate of immigration, an interesting contrast with the American results. Perhaps this is because of the greater diversity of the US – when an American moves to a relatively high-immigration neighbourhood they will come into contact with more immigrants than someone would on moving into a relatively high-immigration neighbourhood in Britain. Alternatively, it might be because our UK analysis uses a smaller neighbourhood unit.[79]

[77]See Hopkins (2009) for the confidence intervals.

[78]The possibility that the coefficient for immigration has declined instead of rising is considered by Hopkins (2009), but attracts a p-value of 0.03 – implying that it can be rejected with 97 per cent certainty.

[79]For the 2005 British analysis we define the neighbourhood in terms of the Lower Layer Super Output Areas in the census, which have an average of 1,513 people. In the US we use counties instead, which are typically vastly more populous.

Whatever the explanation, in the UK in 2005, being well-educated and living near others who are well-educated both sharply reduced anxiety about immigration. By contrast, identifying as a Conservative tended to sharply increase it, although this figure is not shown on the chart as it changed little during the campaign. More interesting, however, is the case of Labour identifiers. Before the election their status is associated with being somewhat more concerned about immigration than the average voter. But after a campaign in which the Conservatives were trying to win over swing voters over the issue of immigration, being a Labour identifier tended, if anything, to reduce concern. This might suggest that those who started out with an anti-Tory orientation were less susceptible to the Conservative campaign.

Few factors, however, saw their predictive power change as markedly during the campaign as local immigration. Previously, its level had no meaningful relationship with anxiety, but after the election it had become a significant predictor of it. By contrast, every other factor which started out having no clear impact continued to have an ambiguous effect after the election.

Among these insignificant factors, curiously, was *change in immigration* in the neighbourhood. In the US, recall that the number of newcomers arriving recently did exert power over how concerned local citizens were – a power independent of the total number of immigrants. For whatever reason, it does not seem to have any similar power in Britain. Before jumping too quickly to speculate on why this may be, it is as well to caution that the measures are defined slightly differently, with the UK measure being restricted to immigration over the last year, which may be too short a time period for citizens to notice. But if we are picking up a genuine difference, it might be that Britons, less culturally accustomed to assimilating newcomers than Americans, draw little distinction between immigrants who have settled and those who arrived only recently – and so have no independent response to new as opposed to settled migrants.

Who gets framed?

Are all immigrants equal, or are some more equal than others? From the pogroms in Caligula's Alexandria to the thuggish vogue for

'Paki-bashing' in 1970s England, history teaches us that particular minorities bear the brunt of particular hatred at particular times. Having established that local conditions and national framing combine to shape public opinion towards immigration in general, we now turn to consider how the same mix of forces might come together to determine attitudes towards particular groups. We do so using a run of four Gallup polls taken in Britain during the 1980s.[80] Preceding the subsequent surge in asylum claims and Eastern European immigration, this gives us a context in which the overwhelming majority of immigrants could be divided into a few discrete groups – principally Irish, Afro-Caribbean, Pakistani and Indian – so that we can consider their effects on attitudes separately.

As we saw in Chapter 3, South Asians – both Pakistanis and Indians – have shown a tendency to cluster in enclaves in Britain. Crude threat theory implies that this would make these groups particularly likely to attract resentment. In line with the Powellite suggestion that 'numbers are of the essence', it predicts that in the face of clustering, local communities would become concerned about ceding control of resources. We have also seen that – at least when compared to South Asians – Afro-Caribbean immigrants have dispersed relatively widely across working-class Britain. The crude theory suggests that this should make them less of a threat.

In 1980s Britain, though, attitudes to immigrants did not play out this way. Complicating the story, once again, are the nationwide political debates. The media frames the debates, and – unsurprisingly – it tends to be more excited by flashes of sensation than the prosaic realities of day-to-day life. The Afro-Caribbean riots in Brixton in 1981 were certainly sensational – dozens of police cars and buildings burned. In 1985 disorder returned to the same streets, with the police losing control for 48 hours, and, in the same year, there was another riot at Broadwater Farm, north London, in which one police officer was stabbed to death. All of this attracted great coverage, forging a link in the public mind connecting West Indian youths to disorder (Solomos, 1993).

---

[80]A total of 4,013 individuals were interviewed in the four surveys; the first in 1983 and the last in 1990.

Overall, only 2.5 per cent of the voters polled by Gallup describe immigration as the country's top problem – a small fraction, reflecting both the range of other contentious issues facing Britain at the time and, perhaps, the fact that the rate of immigration was relatively low at the time. That makes a stark contrast with 2005, when – after the election – one in five voters named immigration as the country's top problem. Nonetheless we can again use regression analysis to establish *which* factors made this small minority so concerned with immigration.[81] The twist this time is that we control separately for the number of people from *different immigrant groups* living in the neighbourhood.[82] Other factors controlled for at the individual level are sex, age, social class and employment status. We also control for the year of the survey and the rate of unemployment in the district.

Figure 6.5 charts the most interesting of the results. For most of the factors, the statistical tests run by Hopkins (2009) suggest there is no meaningful relationship at all. Neither the number of Asians nor the number of Irish people living nearby makes a meaningful difference to an individual's chance of being extremely concerned with immigration; indeed the chart suggests that if there is any effect at all from living near these groups it tends to be negative. But when – all else being equal – an individual moves from an area with relatively few Afro-Caribbeans to an area where they are relatively plentiful, their chance of deeming immigration to be Britain's biggest problem rises by 0.7 percentage points. That might not sound a lot, but the positive relationship is statistically significant – with the link being positive at every point within our margin of error. And because the overall likelihood of any voter being extremely concerned about immigration within our sample is so small, the 0.7 points figure represents a substantial proportional increase in this chance, a rise of more than a quarter.

The chart also shows the effect of being a Labour voter, one of the only variables that turn out to make a significant impact on the

[81]The chance of any individual rating immigration as the top issue counts as a rare event in statistical terms, so the analysis that follows is performed using a logistic regression with a 'rare event' correction.

[82]Neighbourhood is defined as parliamentary constituency in this analysis.

Figure 6.5 Selected drivers of concern with immigration in 1980s Britain

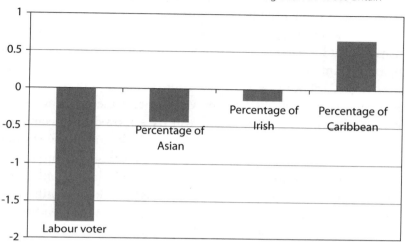

Notes: Percentage point change in the likelihood of a respondent calling immigration the nation's biggest problem when – holding all else equal – he or she shifts from a relatively low value (tenth percentile) to a relatively high value (90th percentile) for each of the indicators shown. For yes/no variables such as 'is Labour supporter', the shift will typically be from 'no' to 'yes'.

likelihood of being concerned with immigration in the 1980s. From the chart it appears that the reduction in concern associated with being Labour at that time is more important than the proportion of individuals living locally who were born in the Caribbean. In line with our earlier analysis, however, we have ranked all districts by how many Caribbeans they have got, and have then examined the effect of moving from the bottom end of this table up to a point that is a tenth of the way down from the top. But given that this minority population was relatively small in the 1980s, even one-tenth of the way down from the top of the table Caribbeans represent just 1.5 per cent of the population. If instead we consider the district that is one-twentieth of the way down from the top of the table, the proportion of Caribbean-born individuals rises to 3.4 per cent. When all else is equal, moving from somewhere with few Caribbeans to such a place increased the chance of harbouring grave concerns by 1.9 percentage points, an increase which constitutes more than two-thirds of the average chance (2.5 per cent) of any individual voter harbouring such concerns – an effect that is more powerful than any other we have examined for Britain at that time.

As well as determining who is anxious about immigrants, debate played out at the national level thus determines which particular groups of immigrants cause the most worry. We have shown that living near Afro-Caribbeans was the cause for particular anxiety in 1980s Britain, but the debates have moved on, and there is now every reason to suspect that suspicions will have moved on in tandem. After 9/11 and London's own terrorist attacks in 2005, anti-Muslim rhetoric became far more prominent and, increasingly, suspicions were raised that Muslims did not fit in. Indeed, it has recently been shown that racial threat is highest in neighbourhoods with large Bangladeshi or Pakistani populations – who of course, tend to be Muslim (Bowyer, 2008 and 2009). In the space of less than a generation, the evolving debate about minorities has seen one bogeyman being displaced by another.

Conclusions

The media are a little like fairground mirrors: they reflect real events, but also distort them. In this chapter we have established that – with migration – they can distort public opinion as well. It affects not only how worried people are but also who they are worried about. Spin-savvy politicians can encourage the process through their choice of rhetoric.

The transatlantic results are consistent. First, words are powerful: they *can* stoke up anxiety. But our second major finding is that the extent to which they do so depends on the number of immigrants living locally. Previously indifferent people can be encouraged to notice and then resent immigrants, but they are less likely to give immigration much thought if they never encounter any. This combined approach – linking national debates with local conditions – not only makes sense, but also explains variation in hostility over time (which crude threat theory ignores) as well as variation between different neighbourhoods, that a crass account of the public being brainwashed by a racist media would not be able to do.

Our findings seem robust. They are found in two countries, in two different eras and in three sets of analysis which have defined localities in very different ways. The subtle story that public opinion is affected by the interaction of local realities and media messages also accords with earlier research (Hopkins, 2007). It found a tendency for reduced support for immigration in those American communities which had been rapidly absorbing newcomers at times when immigration was in the news – the early 1990s, the immediate aftermath of 9/11 and 2006 – but not in the late 1990s and in the early years of this century, when immigration dropped down the nation's agenda.

By international standards, racist politics has not been particularly virulent in either Britain or the United States in recent years. Dixiecrats who were blunt about their opposition to desegregation belong to another age, as does the blood-curdling rhetoric of Enoch Powell. Neither nation currently has a politician of national standing who has made xenophobia central to its message in the way that Jean Marie Le Pen does in France. But because diversity is uncomfortable, even gentler expressions of hostility can inflame resentment, making life tougher for immigrants.

7

Tidal generation:
politics and deeper currents
in public opinion

I stand on the shoulders of giants. I thank the Moses generation; but we've got to remember, now, that Joshua still had a job to do. (Senator Barack Obama, March 2007)

If Barack Obama had lived here I would be very surprised if even somebody as brilliant as him would have been able to break through the institutional stranglehold that there is on power. (Trevor Phillips, chair of Britain's Equality and Human Rights Commission, November 2008)[83]

Did everything change – or nothing? As the world marvelled at a black family moving into the White House, contrarians argued the detailed election results showed how racialised American politics remained. On their account, Obama won purely because he was a Democrat, and they believe that – as an African American – he won less handily than other Democrats might have done in 2008. After all, his victory came after eight years of a Republican administration that was, by the end, deeply unpopular. The President himself, however, does not see it in such negative terms. As he made plain on election night, he believes that 'change has come to America'.

The previous chapter explained how the flames of resentment are fanned by the changing winds of political debate. This chapter assesses whether political change really has come about, by shifting the focus from winds of change above the surface to the underlying tides below. It hunts out – in both minority politics and majority opinion – signs of the kind of fundamental shifts *between cohorts* that

---

[83] *The Times*, 8 November 2008. See: www.timesonline.co.uk/tol/life_and_style/men/article5110226.ece

could make sense of Obama's Biblical rhetoric about the historic transition from the Moses to Joshua generation. As well as establishing that Obama's elevation is indeed a sign of generational change, we ask whether there have been parallel changes in the UK which might make a British black leader possible. Or whether instead – as Trevor Phillips suggests – non-white Britons continue to face barriers that are particular to their side of the Atlantic.

No promised land yet... but the long march continues

Amid all the excitement about America's collective act of redemption in electing Obama, it is of course worth remembering that the racial inequalities outlined in previous chapters have not disappeared. Whether one looks at work or housing or education, African Americans still do not enjoy an equal chance in life in their own land. Despite the talk about Moses making way for Joshua there is still a long way to go on the march to the promised land of equality.

However important change at the top may prove, it is certainly not in itself enough to heal deep social divides. Indeed, even within the political system that is the focus of this chapter, America's 2008 general election contained powerful reminders of the continuing salience of race. The breakdown of the vote revealed that 95 per cent of voting African Americans opted for Obama, as against just 43 per cent of whites,[84] making ethnicity a somewhat stronger predictor of partisan voting than it had been in 2004. British experience with another historically under-represented group underlines the point that change at the top does not necessarily reflect – or automatically bring about – wider change in the system.

Margaret Thatcher became leader of the Conservative party in 1975, and the first female Prime Minister in 1979. At that time women MPs constituted a mere 4 per cent of the House of Commons. Yet the election that brought her to power actually brought about a *decline* in the overall number of women elected, as Figure 7.1 reveals. Almost unbelievably, even after Mrs Thatcher's crushing victory in 1983, the

---

[84] Exit poll figures from the *New York Times*: www.elections.nytimes.com/2008/results/president/exit-polls.html

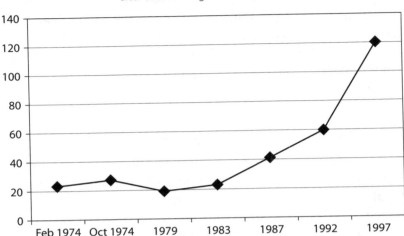

Figure 7.1 No instant Thatcher effect in 1975: women in the Commons after successive general elections

Source: House of Commons Research Papers 01/75 & 05/33

total tally of female MPs remained lower than it had been back in 1945. Her example *may* have given some young women the confidence to try out a career in politics. But although the number of female MPs started to creep up after 1983, it took institutional change (specifically the Labour party's use of all-women shortlists in the mid-1990s) and not just example to bring about the real step change in female representation. It arrived only when the Conservative party, which Thatcher had led until 1990, was roundly defeated in 1997.

There are, however, important differences between the Obama and Thatcher cases. President Obama *does* represent the crest of a wave in a way that Mrs Thatcher did not, in that he arrives in the wake of a sustained rise in the number of black elected officials that can be traced back over several decades. Figure 7.2 charts how their total number across the United States has grown from below 2,000 in 1970 to around 10,000 today. The increase during the 1970s might be interpreted as a delayed response to the civil rights era struggle for the enfranchisement of southern African Americans and the passage of the 1965 Voting Rights Act. Intriguingly, however, the steady increase continued at a similar rate into the 1980s and 1990s, suggesting other forces are at play.

Figure 7.2 Growth at the grassroots: black elected officials in the US and minority ethnic councillors in England

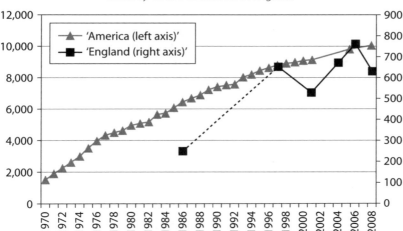

Sources: American figures from Bositis (2003) for 1970–2001 and from Bositis (2008) for 2007. English figures from 1997 onwards from the census of councillors (National Foundation for Educational Research, 2009); figure for 1986 an approximate estimate from Gyford *et al.* (1989), p. 48.

There is no comparably robust series going back so far for England's minority ethnic councillors. But the chart shows that the total roughly doubled to reach around 600 between the mid-1980s and mid-1990s, before oscillating in more recent years. Indeed, it is likely that the growth started before that. As recently as the late 1970s, big multiracial centres such as Birmingham, which now have a large number of minority councillors, lacked any non-white representation. No clear pattern is visible for England over more recent years, but it seems highly likely that an upward underlying trend is being offset by the vicissitudes of party competition. Non-whites are six times better represented among Labour councillors than among the Conservatives[85], and as Labour support has declined since its high watermark in the run-up to Tony Blair's landslide victory in 1997, the number of Labour councillors has declined continually in step.

[85]National Foundation for Educational Research (2009), p. 19.

Population without representation – a very British grievance

So an underlying trend towards greater black representation in the US preceded Obama's rise and seems to be mirrored to some extent in the UK. The next question is whether the rise is as well advanced in Britain. Certainly, the total of 10,000 black elected officials that Figure 7.2 records in contemporary America far exceeds England's 600–750 non-white councillors – even allowing for the fact that there are many more black Americans overall than minority ethnic Britons. But this comparison is not straightforward because of differences in what is being measured on the two sides of the Atlantic.

Most African American elected officials have non-partisan and highly localised roles (Bositis, 2008). The English data in Figure 7.2, however, cover only the principal tier of local government – these councillors represent sizeable wards, control significant budgets and are mostly organised on a formal partisan basis.[86] The two political systems are so different as to make like-for-like comparison impossible. But what we can do is compare the *proportion* of African Americans and English minorities at different levels of office – a comparison presented in Figure 7.3.

At 13 per cent of the overall population, African Americans represent a somewhat but not dramatically higher proportion of the population than do Britain's combined (and broadly defined) minorities. We saw in Chapter 2 that they numbered around 10 per cent of the population in 2001, and also learnt that they will number even more than that today. But the chart shows that they are *much* better represented politically. True, black Americans are not fully represented in either the state legislatures (8.3 per cent) or the US Congress (9.1 per cent), but they are more than half way there. In Britain, by contrast, minority ethnic councillors represent just 3.4 per cent the total, and the 15 minority MPs in Parliament represent an even lower proportion, just 2.3 per cent. It is only in statewide

---

[86] England does also have a lower and more numerous tier of parish councils which might allow for a closer comparison, but these wield minimal power and are largely absent from the Metropolitan boroughs where ethnic minorities are concentrated. As a result, there is little interest in the ethnicity of parish councillors and data on it are not systematically collected.

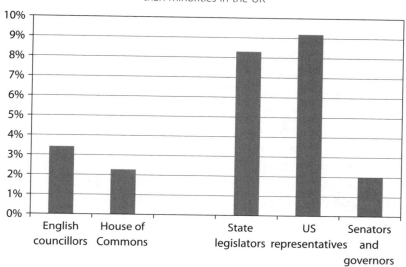

Figure 7.3 African Americans secure a bigger share of political offices than minorities in the UK

Sources: Calculations based on Bositis (2008) for the US, and on National Foundation for Educational Research (2009) for England.

offices – including governors and senators – that African Americans are similarly thin on the ground.

In terms of political representation, then, it seems fair to say that – even before Obama took centre stage – African Americans had progressed considerably further than Britain's ethnic minorities. The next task is to explain that relative American success.

Cultural differences are no doubt part of the picture. The African American community is long-established and has institutions, notably the church, which lend it a cohesiveness that Britain's disparate minorities do not collectively possess. (Indeed to speak of a British minority community – as opposed to communities – is something of a misnomer). Also important is the fact that the struggle for civil rights took place within living memory. That struggle not only created a cadre of leaders, but also forged a collective black American consciousness that is lacking in Britain. That consciousness is evident in the fact that uneducated and poor American blacks register to vote more frequently than their white counterparts.

One study in the 1980s suggested the least-educated American blacks were some 19 percentage points more likely to register than the least-educated whites (Williams, 1987). Other analysis confirms that – once allowance is made for social and economic factors – blacks have long been at least as likely, and sometimes more likely, to turn out to vote than whites.[87] And in the case of 2008, exit polls suggest that a surge of enthusiasm for Barack Obama increased African Americans' share of the total vote to 13 per cent.[88]

Turnout, however, cannot explain transatlantic differences in representation. The 13 per cent vote share in 2008 is broadly in line with the overall share of the population that African Americans represent. The more general pattern has been for blacks to vote *significantly less often overall* than whites. Despite the *relatively* high turnout of African Americans when compared to others at the bottom of the heap, the poor – who are, of course, disproportionately black – still turn out much less often than the affluent. In Britain, by contrast, while ethnic minorities are under-represented on the electoral register, once they are signed up then South Asians, at least, are actually more likely to cast their vote than whites (Fieldhouse and Cutts, 2009).

If it is not turnout, then what can explain the great gulf in minority representation that divides the two sides of the Atlantic? Curiously, a clue is provided by the one American bar in Figure 7.3 which did point to acute black under-representation – that for governors and US senators. At the time of writing, there is only one African American senator out of 100, and of 50 governors only two are black. Of this trio only one, Governor Deval Patrick of Massachusetts, was elected to their current position in his own right. In statewide elections, African Americans have enjoyed – if anything – proportionally less success than minority ethnic Britons in the House of Commons. The track record of relative success of African Americans in the House of Representatives and in state legislatures turns out to be chiefly down to brute political mechanics – the interplay of racial residential segregation with the drawing of district boundaries.

---

[87]See for instance: Verba and Nie (1987) or Wolfinger and Rosenstone (1980).

[88]Exit poll data on minorities in recent elections are collated at: www.nonprofitvote.org/voterturnout2008#minorities

These local factors come out in the wash during a statewide – or nation-wide – election.

Of constituency and concentration

Chapter 3 showed that African Americans were set apart geographically in a manner unmatched by any other major ethnic group within America, or, for that matter, Britain. While this segregation is disadvantageous in all sorts of ways, under the first-past-the-post electoral system used in both the UK and the US, it is also a potential source of political strength. When a minority is concentrated in particular places, it will often constitute a plurality of votes locally, something that never happens for those ethnic groups, such as Afro-Caribbeans in Britain, that are scattered more widely. Indeed, we saw in Chapter 3 that the overwhelming majority (some 84 per cent according to Figure 3.1a) of British non-whites lived in neighbourhoods where they are in the minority locally.

The difference in transatlantic demography is reinforced by differences in how political boundaries are set. For the most part, the US allows the states – in practice most often state legislatures – to draw their own political maps. But since the passage of the Voting Rights Act and particularly its amendment in 1982, the courts have had a role in ensuring the process did not involve racial discrimination. For better or worse, they have often discharged this responsibility by enforcing the creation of more districts where minorities are in the majority. The British system could not be more different. Independent bodies – which keep their distance from party politicians – are charged with settling the borders of council wards and parliamentary constituencies. The over-riding concern is ensuring that any changes equalise the number of voters in each seat, with scope around the edges to relax this rule only if boundaries become so artificial as to undermine community identity.[89] Ethnicity never comes into it. Faced with submissions that race should be considered in

---

[89] For a summary of the rules used in apportioning parliamentary constituencies, see the booklet prepared by the Boundary Commission for England during its 2001 review. Available at: www.statistics.gov.uk/pbc/downloads/pbc_review2001/Allbook.doc

redrawing Leicester's seats in 2004, one of the assistant parliamentary boundary commissioners reaffirmed the colour-blind approach, arguing that drawing up constituencies on the basis of race would be dangerously divisive.[90]

The link between all of this and the growth of the black political class is starkly seen in the US House of Representatives. In 2001, two-thirds of black congressmen came from districts where African Americans were in the majority, and all but one represented districts with more black people than the national average (Bositis, 2002). Ten black congressmen, it is true, had been elected in places where blacks constituted less than 40 per cent of the voting age population. But seven of these represented places where Hispanics, Asians and blacks together outnumbered whites. Thus majority-minority politics sustains *almost all* of the federal echelon of the black political class. It is important at the state level too, with a large proportion of the recent increase in black legislators – up from 423 in 1990 to 622 in 2007 – reflecting the creation of new seats where minority voters held great sway, created in the aftermath of the 1982 reforms (Bositis, 2008).

In Britain, by contrast, minorities lack an equivalent stronghold. Official analysis of the 2001 census suggested that only nine parliamentary constituencies were majority-minority, a mere 1.4 per cent of the then total number of seats.[91] Another seven constituencies were so close to having non-white majorities that they may well have acquired them since (Office for National Statistics, 2003).[92] But even with all these included, minority voters would only control 2.4 per cent of all seats. That figure just happens to match the proportion of seats currently filled by non-white MPs. Six of the current crop of 15 – that is 40 per cent of the total – are crammed into the 2.6 per cent of seats with the highest concentration of non-whites,[93]

[90]His report is available at: www.statistics.gov.uk/pbc/review_areas/leicester.asp

[91]Brent North, Brent South, Camberwell & Peckham, Ealing Southall, East Ham, Ilford South, West Ham, Birmingham Ladywood and Birmingham Sparbrook & Small Heath.

[92]The following constituencies were recorded as being 45 per cent or more non-white: Bethnal Green & Bow, Brent East, Croydon North, Poplar & Canning Town, Birmingham Perry Bar, Leicester East and Bradford West.

[93]The six are: Dawn Butler, Virendra Sharma, Keith Vaz, Khalid Mahmood, Marsha Singh, and David Lammy. The constituency each represents had a non-white population of at least 44.9 per cent in 2001 (Office for National Statistics, 2003).

while another two non-white MPs also have exceptionally diverse constituencies.[94] Thus although Britain's few minority ethnic politicians may not be *quite* as dependent on a racial base as their more numerous American counterparts, most still do depend on one. The most obvious reason why there are so many fewer non-white politicians in Britain is that the combination of demographics and the electoral laws means there are fewer racial bases to be had.

The aim of the creation of majority-minority districts in the United States was a noble one – to stamp out the process of 'cracking', whereby states who had been reluctantly obliged to let their black citizens vote after 1965 responded by splitting up the African American vote into several districts to prevent a black majority. We have seen that it has also had positive effects, through the creation of a black political class that is not matched in Britain. There was, however, a downside – and not just the disfigurement of the map produced by the peculiarly shaped 'Bullwinkle' district that gave New York Hispanics a local majority, or the even more bizarre 'Mark of Zorro' constituency in Louisiana which produced a plurality of black votes.

Faced with North Carolina's winding 12th district – whose extremely peculiar borders had been designed to engineer a black majority – Supreme Court Justice Sandra Day O'Connor described the situation as bearing 'an uncomfortable resemblance to political apartheid'.[95] Racially homogenised seats may achieve a decent level of black representation, but they also ensure that the great bulk of white politicians need give little heed to African American concerns. Arguably, they have also tended to put a cap on black ambitions, by encouraging a racialised politics that played well in the ghetto but went down less well elsewhere. Thus between the 1970s and the 1980s – at exactly the same time as black representation of black districts was surging ahead in the South – the minuscule proportion of majority-white seats in southern legislatures represented by African Americans actually *declined*, from 2 per cent to 1 per cent (Handley and Grofman,

[94]In 2001, more than one in four people living in the constituencies now held by Diane Abbott and Sadiq Khan were non-white (Office for National Statistics, 2003).
[95]Cited in Bybee (1998), p. 127.

1994). Worse, the careful statistical analysis of David Lublin confirmed that the chance of an African American victory in white majority districts fell away rapidly as the black vote declined. Looking at the years 1972 to 1994 he found that 'blacks won only 72 of the 5,079 elections held in white majority districts', and that in the great bulk of even these rare cases Latinos and blacks together constituted the majority.[96]

While this racialised pattern of politics persisted, it was hard to imagine a non-white individual winning through in a nationwide election. The next section explores how far the pattern has changed. Up until the 1990s, though, we have seen that majority-minority politics left the black political class – like much of the community it represents – consigned to the ghetto. And well before the close of the twentieth century, scholars were warning that black politicians were close to exhausting the potential opportunities available in majority-black constituencies (Swain, 1993). The only way to maintain momentum was to move beyond the ghetto of black politics and on to the statewide scene, and indeed the national stage. That is the challenge that fell to the ascendant generation of African American politicians. Foremost among them is Barack Obama.

Moses and Joshua

Moses is one of the Bible's giants because he led the children of Israel out of bondage in Egypt. It was no mean feat, a gruelling task that involved spells in the wilderness and the parting of the Red Sea. By describing civil rights era activists as the 'Moses generation', Obama is saying that their feats were comparably heroic – and comparably difficult. But by invoking Joshua – Moses's heir as ruler of the promised land – he suggests that now is the time for a new generation of black leaders. Such men and women will not have grown up consigned to the back of the bus, as older African American southerners did. Despite the continuing material hardship of much of the black community, the younger cohort have enjoyed much greater opportunities than their parents.

[96]Lublin (1999), pp. 183–184. See also Lublin (1997a and 1997b).

That opportunity, according to one shrewd observer of African American politics, has produced ambitions to go beyond the limitations of sectional politics (Ifill, 2009). She weaves together the story of Barack Obama – who set his sight on statewide election to the US Senate after six years representing the majority-minority 13th district of Illinois's upper house – with that of other up-and-coming black politicians. Among them are Cory Booker, the 40-year-old mayor of Newark, New Jersey, and the 42-year-old Representative Artur Davis, who had to fight off charges from older politicians that he was 'not black enough' before he could prevail in Alabama's majority-minority seventh congressional district. Then there is Deval Patrick, America's one black governor elected in his own right in Massachusetts, a state with many fewer African Americans than the national average.

All these men possess degrees from Ivy League universities, just one sign of the opportunity they have enjoyed. But this elite is only one part of a sudden drift away from sectional politics. Figure 7.4 shows how the number of black state legislators representing non-minority districts has grown sharply in recent years. Across America as a whole, the proportion serving white majority districts has roughly doubled in the last 15 years or so, and even in the South – with its poisonous legacy of racialised politics – there has been a comparable proportional increase, albeit from a lower base.

Of course, African American politicians are still mostly concentrated in black areas, but the rapid shift in the kind of seat that dozens of them represent is too marked to put down to chance. Combined with the continuing growth in the total number of black state legislators, up from 423 in 1990 to 622 in 2007, the most obvious effect has been to sharply increase the number of white Americans who are used to being represented by black people. There is also, however, an effect upon black politics itself, as it learns to grapple with a less homogeneous constituency. The shift from 'protest to politics' in black leadership in the aftermath of the civil rights era is already well documented (Smith, 1990). The growing band of black legislators in white districts embodies a second shift, from one sort of politics to another. The ascent of Barack Obama suggests this second shift is proving just as profound.

Figure 7.4 The growing proportion of African American state legislators who represent non-minority districts

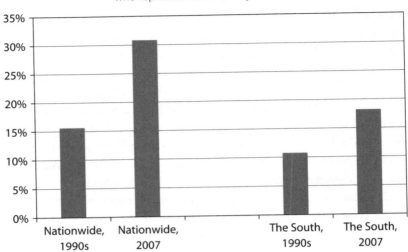

Sources: 2007 figures derived from Bositis (2008); southern 1990s figure from Bositis (1995); nationwide 1990s figure calculated from Table 2.4 in King-Meadows and Schaller (2006), which in turn uses data from Lilley et al. (1997).
Notes: Nationwide 1990s figure is for 1997. The southern 1990s figure is for immediately after the districting process during that decade. Non-minority districts are defined for the 1990s nationwide figure as those districts where the combined percentage of the voting age population that is African American or Hispanic is less than 50 per cent. All other points in the chart are calculated directly from Bositis (2008 and 1995) and so rely upon his definitions.

Theories are fast emerging to try and explain why national black leadership, unthinkable a generation ago, has now become a reality. One, put forward by the journalist Michael Tomasky, centres on the rapid demographic change that we set out in Chapters 1 and 2. He suggests that the 'crucial lesson' of 2008 is the growing power of minority voters, power which he insists can only grow further as the population share of non-Hispanic whites dwindles further, from 68 per cent of America's population today to around half by 2050 (Tomasky, 2008).

The trouble with this argument is that it takes little account of America's most salient colour line. Increasing diversity has not come about because of growing numbers of African Americans: their population share has been relatively stable for several decades. Rather, it reflects the arrival of Asians and Hispanics who – as we have documented throughout this book – fall on the other side of America's deepest racial divide. It is not just that the life chances of African Americans are especially poor when compared to all but the newest immigrants, but also that – as Chapter 3 showed – other minorities tend to regard blacks as undesirable neighbours. While it is true both that Obama built an impressive lead among Hispanics and that an increased Latino vote share in congressional districts can boost black candidates,[97] demography will not do as a general explanation. That is partly because whites retain a crushing majority, and partly because Americans from minorities think of themselves as Asian, Hispanic or black – rather than 'non white'.

A second approach is to search out sociological seeds for Obama's political victory in the growth of a black middle class. When we have uncovered so much evidence of continuing African American disadvantage, any suggestion that *The Cosby Show* or the film *Love Jones* typified black experience in the post-civil rights era would clearly be a mistake.[98] But although African Americans remain disadvantaged overall, official figures show that economic inequality among them has risen especially sharply.[99] So alongside deepening poverty at the bottom end has indeed come an emergent middle class. Successive censuses show that the proportion of black men holding the top graded 'professional' jobs increased from 2 per cent in 1940 to 9 per cent in 1990, with an increase for women over the same period from 4 per cent to 16 per cent. At the same time, the proportion of physicians, lawyers and writers who are black has risen sharply, albeit from a low base.[100]

Together with a quintupling since 1960 in the proportion of African Americans with some experience of college, the increasing prevalence of well-to-do blacks might have been expected to diminish the political centrality of race as a dividing line. For as the economic fortunes of the black community become more mixed, upwardly mobile potential leaders may start to find that they have more in common

[97]Lublin (1999).

[98]Marsh *et al.* (2007) defined the term 'Love Jones generation' to refer to young blacks who were both childless and middle class.

[99]US Bureau of the Census information, reported in Hochschild (1995), p. 49.

[100]Figures in this paragraph from: US Bureau of Census (1943), Table 6; and US Bureau of Census (1992), Table 1.

with white families in better parts of town than fellow African Americans who are left stuck in the ghetto. Might this be why growing numbers of black politicians are making their pitch to whites as well as blacks? The suggestion seems feasible enough, but turns out to lack much power. A whole clutch of studies have explored the link between race and class, and found that race loses none of its importance in the politics of African Americans who climb the class ladder.[101] Michael Dawson, for instance, found that: 'Class divisions were not found to significantly structure African American participation or affect evaluations of which party best advances black interests'. In fact – in direct contradiction to crude predictions based on class self-interest – he found that more prosperous black Americans were especially likely to support the Democrats.[102]

If neither demographics nor sociology can fully explain the arrival of generation Joshua, then we must look elsewhere. Neither the growth of Hispanics nor the black middle class could result in a black man becoming President if the white majority remained as stubbornly racist as they have been in the past. To truly understand what made Obama possible we need to look beyond the generational shift in the African American community and inspect how attitudes are shifting over the generations across Americans as a whole.

The deep tide of tolerance

The deepest forms of racial prejudice are close to home – concerning who people are happy to work and live with. A body of research in the US has long charted the desire to maintain social distance from other racial groups, and has shown this is closely connected to other forms of prejudice.[103] More recently, it has been shown that the desire for social distance is also the rock upon which wider intolerance is built in the UK. Britons who dislike the idea of marrying a non-white are far more likely to be intolerant of everything from traditional dress for immigrant children to financial aid for their parents. Individuals

[101]See for instance: Dawson (1994); Hochschild (1995); Kinder and Sanders (1996).
[102]Dawson (1994), p. 121.
[103]See, for instance: Bogardus (1967), Firebaugh and Davis (1989) and Kleg and Yamamoto (1998).

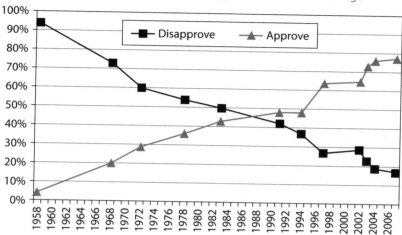

Figure 7.5 Americans increasingly approve of interracial marriage

Source: Gallup. Available at www.gallup.com/poll/28417/Most-Americans-Approve-Interracial-Marriages.aspx

Note: There are some changes in the exact question asked over time; see the above link for details.

who are most uncomfortable with the idea of working for a minority ethnic boss are only half as likely to support anti-discrimination laws as those who do not mind (Ford, 2008). If we can find a *reliable* gauge of the desire for distance between the races in the social sphere, we would thus be well on the way to understanding what is happening to political prejudice too.

The best place to start is mixed race marriage, something surveys have often asked about in both Britain and the US. The American data, however, go back further – for over half a century – so we will start with this. Figure 7.5 charts the answers from the Gallup poll, and – on the face of it – shows an extraordinary trend towards tolerance. Back in the 1950s more than nine Americans in ten (94 per cent) told the pollster that they were opposed to mixed race marriage, but by 2007 more than three-quarters (77 per cent) expressed the opposite view. The data from intermediate years suggest that this wholesale turnaround in public opinion took effect continuously throughout the 50 years.

The impact of this extraordinary chart is reinforced by considera-
tion of the long-term trend towards tolerance in replies to a variety
of polling questions reported by Schuman *et al.* (1997).[104] And its
political importance is underlined by the parallel increase that Gallup
reports in the proportion of Americans who would be willing to vote
for a black President – up from 53 per cent in 1967 to 94 per cent
40 years later.[105] It is thus tempting to glance at the graph and
quickly conclude that Barack Obama was carried to power on a deep
tide of American tolerance.

Unfortunately, nagging doubts remain about how far it can be
trusted. Firstly, the Gallup question is pitched in somewhat abstract
terms – white Americans may have learned to be content with the
idea of mixed race marriage in theory, but what about the more con-
crete question of how they would feel if it were a prospect in their
own family? Fortunately, other surveys in both Britain and America
have put the question this way, asking how respondents would feel
if a black person married a close family member. The results for white
respondents[106] are charted in Figures 7.6a and 7.6b. For the British
case, 7.6a also records how white people feel about the idea of personally having to work for a non-white boss.

Frustratingly, the data cover slightly different periods on the two
sides of the Atlantic. In 1996, one of the two years where we do have
data for both countries, the charts show discomfort with mixed race
marriage is rather more marked among white Americans than white
Britons – running at 43 per cent in the US compared to 35 per cent

---

[104]For example, they report the proportion of Americans agreeing that black and white students should attend the same schools rose from 32 per cent in 1942 to 96 per cent in 1995;
the proportion opposing deliberate efforts to segregate increased from 39 per cent in 1963 to
86 per cent in 1996; and the proportion agreeing that black and white candidates should have
equal chances for jobs rose from 45 per cent in 1944 to 97 per cent in 1972.

[105]Gallup data reported at: www.gallup.com/poll/26611/Some-Americans-Reluctant-Vote-
Mormon-72YearOld-Presidential-Candidates.aspx. The apparent trend for tolerance can be
traced back even further using a question on willingness to vote for a Jewish President, something asked in 1937 when – presumably – the notion of a black President seemed too distant
to make the question relevant. The proportion willing to vote for a Jewish President rose from
46 per cent in 1937 to 82 per cent in 1967 and 92 per cent in 2007.

[106]The American series also excludes white Hispanics on the grounds that – as a
minority – their attitudes to interracial marriage might be expected to be different from
other whites'.

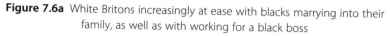

Figure 7.6a White Britons increasingly at ease with blacks marrying into their family, as well as with working for a black boss

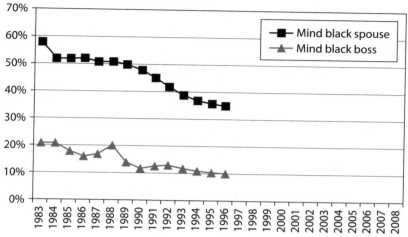

Figure 7.6b White Americans grow more comfortable with blacks marrying into their family at similar rate

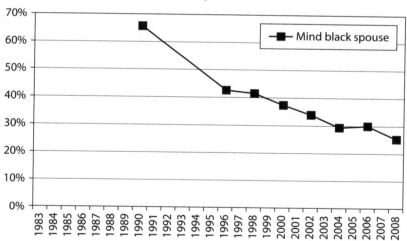

Sources: UK data from Ford (2008) based on British Social Attitudes Survey, 1983–96;
US data from the General Social Survey.
Note: The wording of the marriage questions are very similar, although the British
formulation refers to a 'close relative' while the American one only to a 'family member'.
If anything, this might increase British opposition relative to the reference to 'close' relatives.
For the purposes of this chart 'white Americans' includes non-Hispanic whites only.

in the UK. Nonetheless, it seems quite clear that something similar is going on – a pattern of steady decline. The rate of decline is shown to be broadly comparable. A diminishing desire for social distance also comes through in the British data on the proportion of respondents who would personally resent working for a black boss. This resentment was never as marked as resistance to interracial marriage, but it is nonetheless shown to decline in step.

Contrasting the American data in Figure 7.6b with the Gallup data in Figure 7.5 reveals that bringing the issue of race up close and personal does make a difference. In 1990, for example, 7.6b records 66 per cent discomfort with marriage in one's own family, which compares with the mere 42 per cent who told Gallup one year later that they disapproved of the idea of interracial marriage. But even this change in the focus of the question does not deal with all the possible doubts. The trends seen in 7.6a and 7.6b could be a sign that both Britons and Americans have grown embarrassed about admitting to racial prejudice. The encouraging evidence could, in a well-worn phrase, be a product of mere 'political correctness'.

The philosopher Wittgenstein suggested that buying several copies of the morning paper was no way to ensure that what it said was true.[107] At first blush it may seem that trying to use survey data to prove that people mean what they say when talking to surveys is equally awry. But we can in fact learn a lot about the way in which attitudes have changed by looking at *who* admits to prejudice. In particular, if a taboo on racism is a mere *attitude* affected to fit in with the times, then we might expect that different age groups would pick up on that social pressure to similar extents. If, on the other hand, prejudice (or the lack of it) were a *value* of the hard-to-shift variety – the sort of thing picked up in childhood and not easily unlearnt – then it is likely that *generational change* underlies the apparent tide of tolerance. Box 7.1 expands on this distinction between generational and other forms of age-related change, before we start to put this theory to the test.

---

[107] Wittgenstein, Ludwig (1953) *Philosophical Investigations*. Oxford: Basil Blackwell.

Box 7.1   Disentangling cohort effects from the effect of getting old

All sorts of things tend to happen to us as we get older, the onset of long-sightedness being an obvious example. The old people of today are more long-sighted than their children, and are similarly long-sighted to the old people of a generation ago. Without a breakthrough in optical science it seems likely that when the next generation reaches old age it will be similarly long-sighted too. Sometimes it is suggested that certain political attitudes shift in the same predictable way for every generation, as it develops in experience. The old adage that 'if a man is not a socialist at 20 he has no heart, but if he is still a socialist at 40 he has no head', for instance, embodies the (questionable) idea that the cooling of political passion is a natural part of growing up. If racial intolerance were simply something that comes on with old age we might expect the 'intolerance gap' between a 70-year-old and a 40-year-old would stay relatively constant: so the gap between someone 70 (born in 1910) and someone 40 (born in 1940) in 1980 would be similar to the gap between a 70-year-old (born in 1930) and a 40-year-old (born in 1960) in 2000.

Our suggestion, however, is *not* that prejudice, like long-sightedness, automatically comes on with old age. Rather, it is that – like having been conscripted into the army – racial intolerance might be something associated with having been born before a particular time. In particular, it might affect Britons whose values were forged before the first wave of mass immigration, or Americans raised before the civil rights era. In that case these cohorts might prove to be *permanently* less tolerant than their children, who came of age at a time when prejudice started being challenged.

Social scientists describe generational changes that depend on date of birth, rather than age, as exhibiting a 'cohort effect'. If a cohort effect is at work with racism, snapshot data would still suggest it was an age-related issue, but the outlook for the future would be very different. The passing of a generation that is inclined to prejudice does not necessarily guarantee that it will be automatically replaced with another which has grown intolerant with old age. It might instead be replaced by a new wave of old people who are inclined to lifelong tolerance. In short, with pure life cycle effects, individuals change, but society as a whole does not, whereas with pure generational effects, individuals don't change, but society as a whole does.

We begin this in Figure 7.7 by looking again at attitudes towards interracial marriage in people's own families. This time, however, we group together all respondents – regardless of when they were asked the question – by the year in which they were born. The evidence of generational change is compelling, and remarkably similar on both sides of the Atlantic. The overwhelming majority of white Britons

Figure 7.7 Respondents born in earlier decades are far more likely to oppose a black spouse marrying into their family

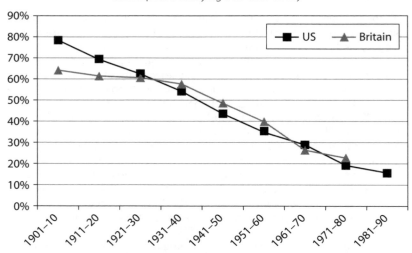

Sources: US data from General Social Survey, 1990–2008; British data from Ford (2008) based on British Social Attitudes Survey, 1983–96.
Note: The white Americans series includes non-Hispanic whites only.

– and even more particularly white Americans – born in the first two decades of the twentieth century were opposed to a black person marrying into the family; for all cohorts born after the 1950s, however, the reverse is true. By the time we get to those generation X-ers who are born in the 1970s, only one in four Britons – and one in five Americans – registers any concern at all.

This pattern of results is not some quirk of this particular marriage question. Ford (2008) shows a parallel inter-generational decline in Britain in the resistance to working for a black boss, which more than halves between those born in the early twentieth century and those born in the 1970s. In America, too, inter-generational increase in tolerance is also found with other questions. One thing gauged repeatedly since the 1970s is the public's reaction to the idea of passing a law against interracial marriage. In this case the generational shift is even more dramatic – support for the idea diminishes from around two-thirds of the Americans born at the tail-end of the nineteenth century to just 3 per cent among the young people of today. Nor is the trend towards tolerance in any way specific to relations between blacks and whites. In Britain, as Ford shows, the signs

Figure 7.8 Evolving opposition among white Americans to a black marrying into the family, measured for two different generations

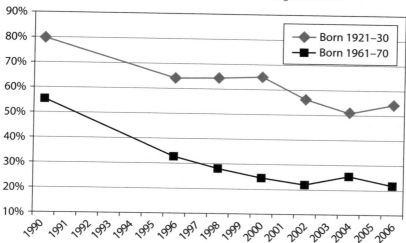

Source: US data from General Social Survey, 1990–2006.

are that exactly the same thing is happening in respect of Asians. And in America, the growing receptiveness of younger cohorts of whites towards the idea of black people marrying into the family is also found when the same question is asked of whites in relation to Asians, Hispanics and Jews.[108]

Generational replacement is not necessarily the only thing going on – people born in different years could also exhibit a *differential* tendency to grow more tolerant with the passing of the years. As an illustration, Figure 7.8 shows trends in opposition to mixed race marriage among Americans born in the 1920s and the 1960s over the period from 1990 through to 2006.[109] It shows not only that

---

[108]Calculations from the General Social Survey. The most notable difference in respect of these minorities, as opposed to African Americans, is that the oldest generations started out with somewhat less hostility towards them.

[109]Data for 2008 suggest a sudden drop in intolerance in that year among the 1920s cohort, a drop so sharp as to make it appear more tolerant than the 1930s cohort. That seems implausible and there are good reasons to think the 2008 data are not meaningful, which is why the chart does not include them. By 2008, survivors from the 1920s are a relative rarity, and so the sample size is very small. In addition those who do survive are increasingly a skewed sample – and skewed towards the upper social classes, something that may bias the results in favour of greater tolerance.

children of the 1960s start out more tolerant than those who came of age during the War years, but also that the gap between the two cohorts actually increases over this time.

Opposition to interracial marriage does decline for the older generation, but not as rapidly as for the young: the *absolute* drop-off for the 1920s cohort is 25 percentage points over the period, as opposed to 33 points for the 1960s generation. And because the younger cohort was less prejudiced to begin with, the *proportional* decline among them is almost twice as big. All this confirms the impression that the younger generations are driving the overall tide of tolerance.

In the case of Britain, Ford (2008) has shown that the tide is pulled more by shifts between generations than anything that happens within them. For the US, Schuman *et al.* (1997) look at all sorts of attitudinal indicators and conclude that 'Each successive cohort is usually more liberal than the one immediately preceding it, and [liberalising] period change occurs gradually'.[110] Their work suggests, in particular, that support for propositions that were most 'challenging' for traditionalists (e.g. support for federally mandated school integration) had risen especially sharply among the very youngest cohorts.

Generational change involves youngsters taking the place of their parents, as their parents die off. Naturally, this tends to be a long and drawn out process. But one would expect the resulting trend towards tolerance to prove permanent.

A determined demon of doubt might still insist that there is a gap between words and deeds. Younger generations, the sceptic may claim, may simply appear far less prejudiced because for some reason they feel more embarrassed about owning up to it than their parents. Fortunately, in the American case, election results can be used to put the sceptical demon to rest. In the past, it is true, there was a tendency to profess willingness to vote for a black candidate before failing to follow through at the polling station. But by analysing some 180 statewide elections that took place between 1989 and 2006, Hopkins (2008) has shown that this gap, which was real as recently

---

[110] See p. 211. The book suggests that period effects are also important alongside the change between cohorts.

as the early 1990s, has now all but disappeared. Voters really are as willing to vote for black politicians as they claim.

The spectacular confirmation of this conclusion came in November 2008 when Barack Obama was elected President, with a margin accurately predicted in the polls. And, in line with our findings here, the new President's support was heavily skewed towards the young.[111] In America, at least, then, the election has proved that what we are witnessing is indeed – in Obama's phrase – change we can believe in. The final section of this chapter considers whether the same is true of Britain.

A British Obama?

Despite the continuing racial divides in America, then, we have seen how a slow tide of tolerance has made possible the election of a black President. At the same time, we have seen how a generation of black politicians – that goes well beyond Barack Obama – has emerged, and is starting to seize the opportunities this change presents. The most obvious question for Britons is whether the same could happen in the UK.

The good news is that in terms of the underlying attitudes of the majority, Britain is in the same place. Close cultural and economic connections between the two nations – and the arguable cultural dependence of Britain on the US – encourage the idea that any deep political tide felt in America will be felt in the UK before long. And all the evidence we have just examined suggests that the deep tide of tolerance is indeed a transatlantic phenomenon. Whether it is willingness to work for a black boss or welcome a non-white person into the family, majority British opinion – just like majority American opinion – is gradually getting more tolerant. And change is taking a similar form on both sides of the Atlantic. Exactly as in the US, the cohort of Britons who wanted social distance from non-whites is gradually dying off, and being replaced by its more tolerant offspring.

---

[111]Exit polls showed Obama leading among the under-30s by an extraordinary margin of two to one: www.elections.nytimes.com/2008/results/president/exit-polls.html

Of all the preconditions for a British Obama, this opinion shift is without doubt the most fundamental. Even more than in America, whites retain a commanding majority of the electorate, and black leadership could only come about with their acquiescence. The political effects of really big social changes, such as the industrial revolution, tend to arrive very slowly. They do not happen *to* us, but instead act *through* us, via the evolution of public opinion. Putnam (1976) documented how industrialisation changed Britain's political class, gradually but irreversibly. It seems entirely plausible that America's civil rights revolution and the increase in diversity being experienced on both sides of the Atlantic will play out in a similar way – slowly, but inexorably.

But if the tide of tolerance is similar in both countries, very different institutions affect the way that tide is felt. Obama successfully used the open system of primaries and caucuses to make young supporters count. In Britain, by contrast, the institutions through which politicians rise to prominence, concentrate power in older hands. First of all, there are the constituency parties that select parliamentary candidates, and their members are mostly older than average. In the 1990s, for instance, a survey suggested the average age of local Conservative members was 62.[112] Secondly, once in parliament, emerging as a leader depends on winning the support of overwhelmingly middle-aged MPs. Although the formal rules of both the Conservative and the Labour party nowadays split responsibility for electing leaders between MPs and rank-and-file members, in a parliamentary system it is near-impossible to emerge as a credible candidate without front-bench experience. Getting that depends on impressing the existing elite. Even if MPs are not themselves prejudiced, if they come from a generation where many people are, they may take a dim view of what a black party leader would mean for the party's prospects.

All these considerations no doubt inform Trevor Phillips's view that a British Barack Obama would not have the chance to get to the top. Various efforts are being made to reform the institutions, notably the so-called 'A-list' of candidates that the Conservatives are imposing

---

[112] Reported in Wright (2000), p. 103.

from head office – as they scramble to achieve a party that looks more like Britain, and one that is less readily caricatured as an overwhelmingly white, male clique. We will not know exactly how much will come of this until after the next election, but the prospects for a sudden surge of minority representation seem dimmer now that the Labour party is reported to have given up on the option of all-black shortlists.[113]

Another institution still missing in Britain is a sizeable black political class. The numbers are so small that it is hard to reach robust conclusions about patterns of change within it, let alone to talk with any confidence about the shift from a Moses to a Joshua generation. Nonetheless, there are a few straws in the wind. The first few non-white MPs in the 1980s – Diane Abbott, Paul Boateng, Keith Vaz, Bernie Grant – were all returned for constituencies with a large proportion of non-white voters, unlike one or two more recent non-white arrivals to the Commons, such as Parmjit Dhanda.

The first few minority ethnic MPs had, to some extent, made their name in black politics, all being intimately involved in the 1980s arguments about whether Labour should have a separate black section. The Conservatives, meanwhile, had no black MPs at all. In 1992 they ran black hopeful John Taylor in the snow-white constituency of Cheltenham. Local party members turned against him and helped elect a Liberal rival. Compare his story with that of Conservative Adam Afryie, who became the first black Tory MP when he triumphed in Windsor in 2005 – a constituency whose mix of white and non-white voters is exactly in line with the national average. Articulate and charismatic, if we put to one side his Conservative brand of politics, Afryie looks like a model member of Obama's Joshua generation.

Obama has, of course, now shown himself to be an exceptionally gifted politician. No minority ethnic British politician has yet had a comparable chance to demonstrate such gifts so fully, and it is possible that none of the small group of those who are currently active are in fact leadership material – although, of course, that cannot be ruled out.

---

[113]*Guardian*, 24 January 2009: www.guardian.co.uk/politics/2009/jan/24/all-black-mp-shortlists

Afryie recently gave his own verdict on the prospects for a British
Obama, telling *The Times*: 'I do not believe we will see a black Prime
Minister in my lifetime'.[114] His reasoning did not turn on public
opinion, which we have seen seems little different from that in the
US. Instead he fixed on the institutional differences we have discussed.
'In the US a fresh face like Obama can make it in one electoral cycle',
Afryie explained. 'In Britain it's generally a gradual process of service
and promotion over many years, and often decades, before leading
a political party'. His argument makes sense, but is it possible he
is overplaying it for superstitious reasons? He must be aware that
Margaret Thatcher said similar things about the prospect of a female
PM just a few short years before she became Tory leader. If a future
British Obama – whether Afryie or anyone else – proves to be anything like the American original, he will surely arrive a little more
quickly than anyone is expecting.

---

[114] *The Times*, 8 November 2008: www.timesonline.co.uk/tol/news/politics/article5110811.ece

8

Concluding thoughts: making a success of the revolution

A choiceless singularity of human identity not only diminishes us all, it also makes the world more flammable. (Amartya Sen, economist and philosopher, writing in 2006)[115]

Britain and America, in common with rich countries around the world, are becoming more diverse. For the immediate future, the continuation of this trend is inevitable, and so in the coming years both countries will become more diverse still. The arrival of immigrants has conferred many benefits – enriching culture, encouraging economic growth and providing the West with a means to address the rapid ageing of the indigenous population. Whatever the accompanying problems, the pertinent debate is not about whether great diversity is desirable or not, but rather about how society can successfully accommodate what is fast becoming established fact.

Both the UK and the US start out with some important advantages in dealing with diversity, and we have seen that some immigrant groups of the last few decades – such as Indians in the UK, and Chinese people in the US – have integrated relatively comfortably into their new homes. As an immigrant nation, the US has a particular tradition of accommodating newcomers from disparate parts of the globe. Irish Catholics, Italians and East European Jews were all integrated into the American mainstream long ago, while still being allowed to hold on to what is distinctive in their culture. The UK has historically been more sheltered from ethnic difference, but the ideals of the post-imperial Commonwealth allowed Indians and Africans to secure full legal and political rights without having to disown their

---

[115]Sen (2007 [2006]), p. 16.

own particular inheritance. Unlike in many European countries, neither Britain nor America is given to thinking that all ethnic distinctions can or should be washed away through some sort of citizenship process.

The past bears upon the present

Both nations, then, are to some extent theoretically accustomed to the idea of living with difference. Their respective experience of it, however, has not always been happy. In the United States, the most particular problems have concerned the conditions of blacks. Forcibly shipped to the New World in the seventeenth and eighteenth centuries, African Americans retain special disadvantages even in the twenty-first century, as we have seen.

While many American immigrant groups fare better than their British counterparts, and even those who face disadvantage tend to see conditions improving after a generation or two, we have shown that African Americans face stubborn disadvantages. For example, we have learnt that:

- African American men are barely half (52 per cent) as likely to be in a 'salariat' profession than white men with similar qualifications
- black Americans die, on average, five years younger than whites
- nearly half (48 per cent) of all African Americans are consigned to ghettoised black majority neighbourhoods – despite the fact that most would prefer to live in an integrated community

The arrival of Barack Obama will not reverse these hard realities any time soon. Similar indicators show that British Muslims, particularly those with roots in Bangladesh or Pakistan, also face particular problems. While not quite ghettoised in the manner of African Americans, British Muslims are nonetheless highly segregated, and live blighted lives in terms of wealth, health and education. Amid inflammatory talk about a global clash between Christendom and Islamic civilisation it hardly needs saying that this creates a particularly worrying situation. The plight of Britain's Muslims can be viewed as one part of a wider transatlantic difference in the nature of immigration and the response to it. In the US, which has a strong tradition of religious pluralism, faith tends to soften the edges of the cleavage between immigrants and native-born Americans. A very high proportion of US immigrants are co-religionists with native-born Americans (Catholics, evangelical Protestants, etc.), and since religion – of whatever form – is important to most Americans, both newcomers and natives, faith tends to blur or even outweigh the immigrant/ non-immigrant distinction. By contrast, a substantial fraction of UK immigrants are devout Muslims, whereas the vast majority of white Britons are emphatically non-devout Christians. As a result, religion arguably tends to divide immigrants from non-immigrants in Britain, whereas it tends to unite immigrants and non-immigrants in the US.

Whereas the most important racial cleavage in America is that which divides blacks from all others, in the UK the divide that counts is between whites and the rest. Whatever challenges the coming of a multi-faith society may pose for Britain, race itself does not cleave a faultline through British society in quite the way that it does in the US. Despite their phenotypical similarities to Bangladeshis and Pakistanis, we have seen that British Indians thrive – British Indian men, for instance, are just as likely to obtain top jobs as are 'similar' British white men. Meanwhile Afro-Caribbeans have assimilated very extensively into the British working class, in terms of both marriage and housing.

But if the US fares less well with race, there are some respects in which British society – whose experience of absorbing migrants is mostly recent – integrates newcomers less well than the immigrant nation of America. We have, for example, established that:

- the ethnic penalty that male immigrants face when it comes to finding a job is around twice as large in Britain as it is in the US
- American immigrants enjoy a health premium, whereas minorities in Britain suffer a health penalty

The contrast also extends to imprisonment, which American – though not British – immigrants are particularly unlikely to face. But it should not be overdone. British immigrants are actually less disadvantaged in securing the top jobs than their American counterparts are on average, although in both countries there are encouraging signs of rising social mobility across the generations.

Transcending 'Them and Us'

'All nice people, like Us are We / And everyone else is a They', Rudyard Kipling famously wrote. To some extent, since time immemorial humans have always been more comfortable dealing with 'like' others – sharing our tribal affiliation, our customs, our culture, our language, our gestures and intonations. While rapidly diversifying nations such as Britain and the US are becoming more comfortable with difference – especially among their young – this evolutionary change, like any evolutionary change, can seem slow in coming.

Moreover, when people live in material conditions that are vastly unalike, they will be more inclined to regard the other as too different from themselves to empathise with. The very inequalities that we have identified thus become a marker of difference in their own right, and so deter integration between racial groups. In particular, the great gulf in living standards between the white majority and those minorities at the bottom of the heap is surely one driver of the discomfort with diversity that we have uncovered on both sides of the Atlantic. The danger is that instead of considering an American black man, for instance, as a father, a worker or a fellow sports fan, some white Americans may classify him primarily as black, and relegate other aspects of his identity to an afterthought. Black people who live at a great social distance from whites may equally view the majority in the same narrow way. British Muslims are likewise at risk of being defined in terms of their religion alone.

This stripping down of identity to the single dimension of religion or ethnicity is what Amartya Sen refers to when he warns against the 'singularity of human identity'. Arguably, this is a greater danger in the United States because of the long history of race as a social dividing line. In Britain, social identities such as class – which can apply across racial lines – may have more importance. Indeed, while we have found that people 'hunker down' in the face of diversity in both countries, the corrosive effect on community living turned out to be more pronounced in America.

Addressing the inequities faced by certain minorities – through anti-discrimination laws and social welfare, for instance – is perhaps the most obvious way to reduce the social distance between racial groups and so encourage empathy between them. Another strategy that could pay dividends is facilitating contact between different ethnic groups.

This is perfectly compatible with the existence of ethnic enclaves. While we have seen that the ghetto can be imprisoning, we have also discovered that in Britain, in particular, minorities can benefit from living alongside members of their own ethnic group. While it seems surprising to some, our research indicates that stronger intra-racial bonds and stronger interracial bridges can be positively, rather than negatively, related. In other words, the same American or Brit who has more ties to others of their *own* racial and ethnic group is actually *more* likely, not less likely, to have more social bridges to other racial and ethnic groups. A hundred years ago social clubs for Italian Americans proved, in the long run, an effective way to integrate Italian immigrants into broader American society, and today black Americans who have more black friends have more (not fewer) white friends. Likewise American whites who trust whites more tend also to trust Latinos more, not less, than whites who distrust whites. To be sure, not all ethnic bonding leads to ethnic bridging; Al Qaeda is a notable exception. Nonetheless, our research tends to support public policies which foster the building of strong bonds *within* ethnic groups (such as Mexican American clubs, or a Chinese British neighbourhood group) because that could be an important prelude to the broader social bridging we seek. Conversely, attempts to bring about bridging by discouraging the markers of bonding – such as Muslim dress, for example – could end up self-defeating by producing isolating alienation.

A social salad bowl is thus a better ideal than a homogenising melting pot, something American society with its long tradition of heterogeneity is arguably more instinctively at ease with than traditionally homogeneous Britain. But the distinct elements of a salad still need to be tossed together, and the priority for policy-makers must be removing barriers to integration. For many immigrants in both Britain and the US, language is the most obvious hurdle. Making it cheap and easy for immigrants who want to learn English to do so, would be a practical way to make them feel more at home – and, at the same time, perhaps, a means of dispelling discomfort about diversity among the indigenous community. Locating sports or youth facilities or libraries where they serve both white and non-white parts of town is the type of small step that could help to break down ethnic boundaries by encouraging informal contact between different ethnic groups. Conversely, our findings raise questions about the wisdom of fostering institutions such as Christian or Muslim faith schools, which the British government has promoted in recent years, which might work to keep different ethnic groups apart.

For politicians and other leaders the *don'ts* are just as important as the *dos*. Above all, there is a duty on them not to inflame potential tensions. From the former Yugoslavia to Rwanda, glib accounts of 'ancient ethnic hatreds' are inevitably wide of the mark. Mistrust between races is a function of the way particular societies are organised – and, very often, a product of manipulation too.[116] Tensions between majorities and minorities in Britain and the US are mercifully less severe. But we have seen that they do respond to the rhetoric of the elite. British public concern about immigration surged in 2005 after the Conservatives emphasised the issue. Opinion likewise hardened in the US the following year after the press latched on to the issue, despite immigration simultaneously declining from its peak. So it's not just sticks and stones but also media words that hurt when it comes to race relations. In Chapter 6 we saw that anti-immigrant rhetoric does the most damage in those communities with more first-hand experience of immigration. Nationwide perceptions of minorities will, however, also have a bearing on whether xenophobia hits home.

The age of Obama

In the case of the United States, perceptions about race are currently being reshaped by Barack Obama. Regardless of how he performs in the highest office, merely by holding it he is sweeping away old ideas about what minorities can and cannot do. But if the President is changing attitudes about race, his rise to power was only possible because change was already well under way.

---

[116]See Glover (1999), particularly pp. 119–122 for an account of how the supposedly ancient mistrust between tribes that gave rise to mass murder in 1990s Rwanda was in fact whipped up using the modern mass media.

We have seen that among America's majority, the current has been running in favour of tolerance for several decades. On the question of mixed race marriage, for example, whereas in the 1950s more than nine Americans in every ten told pollsters that they were against mixed race marriage, more than three in four today insist that they are in favour. Similar trends are evident on other race-related attitudes, and lingering suspicions that they reflect nothing more than 'political correctness' have been answered now that a clear majority of Americans have chosen a black man to lead them.

We have also seen that this change is of a *generational* nature, and looks set to continue as the cohort who grew up before the civil rights struggle continues to be replaced by new generations who have mostly grown up sympathetic to the ideal of racial equality. So the age of Obama did not come out of nowhere, but was carried into being on deep social tides.

The President, it is true, initially rose through the ranks of a black political class that has no equal in Britain. Neither demographics nor districting rules encourage the same scale of minority politics in the UK. But it would be wrong to assume this precludes the emergence of a non-white Prime Minister in the UK. In the end, the President had to win by transcending his own race and relying upon the tolerance of the majority. All the surveys we have reviewed show the same generational tide of tolerance at work in the UK. This, more than anything else, is the crucial precondition for a British Obama arriving to claim the keys to No. 10.

Bibliography

Adler, N. E. and Rehkopf, D. H. (2008) 'US Disparities in Health: Descriptions, Causes and Mechanisms', *Annual Review of Public Health*, 29, 235–252.

Alba, R. D. and Nee, V. (1997) 'Rethinking Assimilation Theory for a New Century', *International Migration Review*, 31, 826–874.

Alba, R. D. and Nee, V. (2003) *Remaking the American Mainstream: Assimilation and Contemporary Immigration*. Cambridge, MA: Harvard University Press.

Allport, G. (1954) *The Nature of Prejudice*. Reading, MA: Addison-Wesley.

Anderson, C. J. and Paskeviciute, A. (2006) 'How Ethnic and Linguistic Heterogeneity Influence the Prospects for Civil Society: A Comparative Study of Citizenship Behavior', *Journal of Politics*, 68(4), 783–802.

Bean, F. D. and Stevens, G. (2003) *America's Newcomers and the Dynamics of Diversity*. New York: Russell Sage Foundation.

Blalock, H. M. Jr (1967) *Toward a Theory of Minority-Group Relations*. New York: Wiley and Sons.

Blumer, H. (1958) 'Race Prejudice as a Sense of Group Position', *Pacific Sociological Review*, 1, 3–7.

Boal, F. W. (1995) *Shaping a City: Belfast in the Late Twentieth Century*. Belfast: Institute of Irish Studies.

Bogardus, E. (1967) *A Forty Year Racial Distance Study*. Pasadena: University of South California Press.

Bositis, D. A. (1995) *Redistricting and Representation: The Creation of Majority-Minority Districts and the Evolving Party System in the South*. Washington, DC: Joint Center for Political and Economic Studies.

Bositis, D. A. (2002) *Black Elected Officials: A Statistical Summary, 2000*. Washington, DC: Joint Center for Political and Economic Studies.

Bositis, D. A. (2003) *Black Elected Officials: A Statistical Summary, 2001*. Washington DC: Joint Center for Political and Economic Studies.

Bositis, D. A. (2008) 'The Political Intermediation Process in the United States: How the American Party System Segregated African American

Interests'. Unpublished mimeo obtained from the author at the Joint Center for Political and Economic Studies in Washington, DC.

Bowyer, B. T. (2008) 'Local Context and Extreme Right Support in England: The British National Party in the 2002 and 2003 Local Elections', *Electoral Studies*, 27(4), 611–620.

Bowyer, B. T. (2009) 'The Contextual Determinants of Whites' Racial Attitudes in England', *British Journal of Political Science*, 39(3), 559–586.

Burgess, S., Wilson, D., Briggs, A. and Piebalga, A. (2008) 'Segregation and the Attainment of Minority Ethnic Pupils in England'. Working Paper No. 08/204, Centre for Market and Public Organisation, University of Bristol.

Bybee, K. J. (1998) *Mistaken Identity: The Supreme Court and the Politics of Minority Representation*. Princeton, NJ: Princeton University Press.

Card, D. and Rothstein, J. (2007) 'Racial Segregation and the Black–White Test Score Gap', *Journal of Public Economics*, 91, 2,158–2,184.

Charles, C. Z. (2000) 'Neighborhood Racial Composition Preferences: Evidence from a Multiethnic Metropolis', *Social Problems*, 47(3), 379–407.

Charles, C. Z. (2003) 'The Dynamics of Racial Residential Segregation', *Annual Review of Sociology*, 29, 167–207.

Cheung, S. and Heath, A. (2007) 'Nice Work if You Can Get it: Ethnic Penalties in Great Britain', in A. Heath and S. Cheung (eds), *Unequal Chances: Ethnic Minorities in Western Labour Markets*. Oxford: Oxford University Press, pp. 505–548.

Chwe, M. (2001) *Rational Ritual: Culture, Co-ordination, and Common Knowledge*. Princeton, NJ: Princeton University Press.

Dawson, M. C. (1994) *Behind the Mule: Race and Class in American Politics*. Princeton, NJ: Princeton University Press.

Denton, N. (1994) 'Are African Americans Still Hypersegregated?', in R. D. Bullard, J. E. Grigsby, C. Lee and J. R. Feagin (eds), *Residential Apartheid: The American Legacy, Vol. 2*. CAAS Urban Policy Series. Los Angeles, CA: CAAS Publications, pp. 49–81.

Dorling, D. and Rees, P. (2003) 'A Nation Still Dividing: The British Census and Social Polarisation 1971–2001', *Environment and Planning A*, 35(7), 1,287–1,313.

Du Bois, W. E. B. (1990 [1903]) *The Souls of Black Folk: Essays and Sketches*. New York: Vintage Books.

Duncan, O. D. and Lieberson, S. (1959) 'Ethnic Segregation and Assimilation', *American Journal of Sociology*, 64(4), 364–374.

Edmonston, B. and Passel, J. S. (1992) 'Immigration and Immigrant Generations in Population Projections', *International Journal of Forecasting*, 8(3), 459–476.

Farley, R., Schuman, H., Bianchi, S., Colasanto, D. and Hatchett, S. (1978) 'Chocolate City, Vanilla Suburbs: Will the Trend toward Racially Separate Communities Continue?', *Social Science Research*, 7, 319–344.

Farley, R., Steeh, C., Krysan, M., Jackson, T. and Reeves, K. (1994) 'Stereotypes and Segregation: Neighborhoods in the Detroit Area', *American Journal of Sociology*, 100(3), 750–780.

Fieldhouse, E. and Cutts, D. (2008) *Electoral Participation of Hindu and Sikh Communities in England and Wales*. London: Hindu Council UK. Available at: www.hinducounciluk.org/newsite/report/Electora_participation.pdf

Fieldhouse, E. and Cutts, D. (2009) 'A Comparative Study of Social Capital and Neighbourhood Composition in the US and England'. Paper prepared for the Harvard-Manchester Initiative on Social Change. Available at: www.ageofobamabook.com/papers/CuttsFieldhouse.pdf

Firebaugh, G. and Davis, K. (1989) 'Trends in Antiblack Prejudice 1972–1984: Region and Cohort Effects', *American Journal of Sociology*, 94(2), 251–272.

Foner, N. and Alba, R. (2008) 'Immigrant Religion in the US and Western Europe: Bridge or Barrier to Inclusion?', *International Migration Review*, 42, 360–392.

Ford, R. G. (1950) 'Population Succession in Chicago', *American Journal of Sociology*, 56(2), 151–160.

Ford, R. (2008) 'Is Racial Prejudice Declining in Britain?', *British Journal of Sociology*, 59(4), 609–636.

Gallup, A. and Newport, F. (2004) *The Gallup Poll: Public Opinion 2004*. Lanham, MD: Rowman & Littlefield.

Glover, J. (1999) *Humanity: A Moral History of the Twentieth Century*. London: Jonathan Cape.

Goldthorpe, J. H., with Llewellyn, C. and Payne, C. (1987) *Social Mobility and Class Structure in Modern Britain*. Oxford: Clarendon Press.

Grenier, P. and Wright, K. (2006) 'Social Capital in Britain: Exploring the Hall Paradox', *Policy Studies*, 27(1), 27–53.

Gyford, J., Leach, S. and Game, C. (1989) *The Changing Politics of Local Government*. London: Unwin Hyman.

Hagan, J. and Palloni, A. (1999) 'Sociological Criminology and the Mythology of Hispanic Immigration and Crime', *Social Problems*, 46(4), 617–632.

Hall, P. (1999) 'Social Capital in Britain', *British Journal of Political Science*, 29(3), 417–461.

Halpern, D. (2005) *Social Capital*. Cambridge: Polity.

Handley, L. and Grofman, B. (1994) 'The Impact of the Voting Rights Act on Minority Representation: Black Officeholding in Southern State Legislatures and Congressional Delegations', in C. Davidson and B. Grofman (eds), *Quiet Revolution in the South: The Impact of the Voting Rights Act*. Princeton, NJ: Princeton University Press, pp. 335–350.

Hauser, P. M. (1958) 'On the Impact of Urbanism on Social Organization, Human Nature and Political Order', *Confluence*, 7(1), 57–69.

Hochschild, J. (1995) *Facing up to the American Dream: Race, Class, and the Soul of the Nation*. Princeton, NJ: Princeton University Press.

Hopkins, D. J. (2007) 'Threatening Changes: Explaining When and Where Immigrants Provoke Local Opposition'. Paper presented at the Annual Meeting of the American Political Science Association, Chicago, IL. Available at: www.people.iq.harvard.edu/~dhopkins/immpap75tot.pdf

Hopkins, D. J. (2008) 'No More Wilder Effect, Never a Whitman Effect: When and Why Polls Mislead about Black and Female Candidates'. Available at: www.people.iq.harvard.edu/~dhopkins/wilder13.pdf

Hopkins, D. J. (2009) 'National Debates, Local Responses: The Origins of Local Concern about Immigrants in the UK and the US'. Paper prepared for the Harvard-Manchester Initiative on Social Change. Available at: www.ageofobamabook.com/papers/Hopkins.pdf

Iceland, J. and Weinberg, D. H., with Steinmetz, E. (2002) *Racial and Ethnic Residential Segregation in the United States, 1980–2000*. Washington, DC: Bureau of the Census.

Ifill, G. (2009) *The Breakthrough: Politics and Race in the Age of Obama*. New York: Random House.

Iyengar, S. and Kinder, D. R. (1987) *News that Matters*. Chicago, IL: University of Chicago Press.

Joppke, C. (1999) *Immigration and the Nation-State*. Oxford: Oxford University Press.

Kasinitz, P. (2004) 'Race, Assimilation and Second Generations: Past and Present', in N. Foner and G. M. Fredrickson (eds), *Not Just Black and White: Historical and Contemporary Perspectives on Immigration, Race, and Ethnicity in the United States*. New York: Russell Sage Foundation, pp. 278–298.

Kavanagh, D. and Butler, D. (2005) *The British General Election of 2005*. New York: Macmillan.

Key, V. O. (1949) *Southern Politics in State and Nation*. New York: A. A. Knopf.

Kinder, D. R. and Sanders, L. M. (1996) *Divided Color: Racial Politics and Democratic Ideals*. Chicago, IL: University of Chicago Press.

King-Meadows, T. and Schaller, T. F. (2006) *Devolution and Black State Legislators: Challenges and Choices in the Twenty-first Century*. Albany, NY: State University of New York Press.

Kleg, M. and Yamamoto, K. (1998) 'As the World Turns: Ethno-Racial Distances After 70 Years', *Social Science Journal*, 35(2), 183–190.

Kyambi, S. (2005) *Beyond Black and White: Mapping New Immigrant Communities*. London: Institute for Public Policy Research.

Laurence, J. and Heath, A. (2008) *Predictors of Community Cohesion: Multi-Level Modelling of the 2005 Citizenship Survey*. London: Department of Communities and Local Government.

Ley, D. (1974) *The Black Inner City as Frontier Outpost: Images and Behavior of a Philadelphia Neighborhood*. Washington, DC: Association of American Geographers.

Li, Y. (2009) 'The Labour Market Situation of Minority Ethnic Groups in Britain and the USA: An Analysis of Employment Status and Class Position (1990/1–2000/1)', forthcoming in *EuroAmerica: A Journal of European and American Studies*.

Li, Y., Savage, M. and Pickles, A. (2003) 'Social Capital and Social Exclusion in England and Wales (1972–1999)', *British Journal of Sociology*, 54(4), 497–526.

Lieberson, S. (1963) *Ethnic Patterns in American Cities*. New York: The Free Press of Glencoe.

Lilley, W., DeFranco, L. J. and Diefenderfer, W. M. (1994) *State Data Atlas: The Almanac of State Legislatures*. Washington, DC: Congressional quarterly inc.

Lublin, D. (1997a) 'The Election of African Americans and Latinos to the US House of Representatives', *American Politics Quarterly*, 25(3), 269–286.

Lublin, D. (1997b) *The Paradox of Representation: Racial Gerrymandering and Minority Interests in Congress*. Princeton, NJ: Princeton University Press.

Lublin, D. (1999) 'Racial Redistricting and African-American Representation: A Critique of "Do Majority-Minority Districts Maximize Substantive Black Representation in Congress?"', *American Political Science Review*, 93(1), 183–186.

Marsh, K., Cohen, P. N. and Casper, L. (2007) 'The Emerging Black Middle Class: Single and Living Alone', *Social Forces*, 86(2), 735–762.

Martinez, R. Jr and Valenzuela, A. (eds) (2006) *Immigration and Crime*. New York: New York University Press.

Massey, D. S. (1995) 'The New Immigration and Ethnicity in the United States', *Population and Development Review*, 21(3), 631–652.

Massey, D. S. and Denton, N. A. (1993) *American Apartheid: Segregation and the Making of the Underclass*. Cambridge, MA: Harvard University Press.

National Foundation for Educational Research (2009) *National Census of Local Authority Councillors 2008*. Slough: NFER.

Nazroo, J. (2003) 'The Structuring of Ethnic Inequalities in Health: Economic Position, Racial Discrimination, and Racism', *Public Health Matters*, 93, 277–284.

Obama, B. (2007) 'Selma Voting Rights March Commemoration'. Speech March 2007. Available at: www.barackobama.com/2007/03/04/selma_voting_rights_march_comm.php

Obama, B. (2008) 'A More Perfect Union'. Speech March 2008 at Philadelphia, Pennsylvania. Available at: www.mybarackobama.com/page/content/hisownwords

OECD (2007) *Trends in International Migration Flows and Stocks, 1975–2005*. OECD Social, Employment and Migration Working Papers, DELSA/ELSA/WD/SEM(2007)13. Paris: Organisation for Economic Co-operation and Development.

Office for National Statistics (2003) *Census 2001: Report for Parliamentary Constituencies*. London: The Stationery Office. Available at: www.statistics.gov.uk/statbase/Product.asp?vlnk=10725

Park, R. E. (1926) 'The Urban Community as a Spatial Pattern and Moral Order', in E. W. Burgess (ed.), *The Urban Community*. Chicago, IL: University of Chicago Press, pp. 3–17.

Passel, J. S. (2005) *Unauthorized Migrants: Numbers and Characteristics*. Washington, DC: Pew Hispanic Center.

Passel, J. S. and Suro, R. (2006) *Rise, Peak, and Decline: Trends in US Immigration, 1992–2004*. Washington, DC: Pew Hispanic Center.

Patterson, O. (2005) 'Four Modes of Ethno-somatic Stratification: The Experience of Blacks in Europe and the Americas', in G. C. Loury, T. Modood and S. M. Teles (eds), *Ethnicity, Social Mobility and Public Policy: Comparing the US and the UK*. Cambridge: Cambridge University Press, pp. 67–122.

Peach, C. (1996) 'Does Britain have Ghettos?', *Transactions of the Institute of British Geographers*, NS 22(1), 216–235.

Peach, C. (2005) 'The Mosaic versus the Melting Pot: Canada and the USA', *Scottish Geographical Journal*, 121(1), 3–27.

Peach, C. (2006) 'Islam, Ethnicity and South Asian Religions in the London 2001 Census', *Transactions of the Institute of British Geographers*, NS 31(3), 353–370.

Peach, C. (2009) 'Contrasts in US and British Segregation Patterns'. Paper prepared for the Harvard-Manchester Initiative on Social Change. Available at: www.ageofobamabook.com/papers/CeriPeachPaper.pdf

Pennant, R. (2005) *Diversity, Trust and Community Participation in England*. Home Office Findings 253, Research, Development and Statistics Directorate. Available at: www.homeoffice.gov.uk/rds/pdfs05/r253.pdf

Phillips, T. (2005) 'After 7/7: Sleepwalking to Segregation'. Address to Manchester Council for Community Relations, 22 September. Retrievable on the website of the (now defunct) Commission for Racial Equality, at: www.83.137.212.42/sitearchive/cre/Default.aspx.LocID-0hgnew07s. RefLocID-0hg00900c002.Lang-EN.htm

Philpott, T. L. (1978) *The Slum and the Ghetto: Neighborhood Deterioration and Middle-Class Reform, Chicago, 1880–1930*. New York: Oxford University Press.

Powell, E. (1968) 'Rivers of Blood'. Speech delivered to a Conservative Association meeting, Birmingham, 20 April 1968. Available at: www.telegraph.co.uk/comment/3643823/Enoch-Powells-River-of-Blood-speech.html

Putnam, R. D. (1976) *The Comparative Study of Political Elites*. Englewood Cliffs, NJ: Prentice Hall.

Putnam, R. D. (2000) *Bowling Alone: The Collapse and Revival of American Community*. New York: Simon & Schuster.

Putnam, R. D. (2007) 'E Pluribus Unum: Civic Engagement in a Diverse and Changing Society', *Scandinavian Political Studies*, 30(2), 137–174.

Schelling, T. C. (1971) 'Dynamic Models of Segregation', *Journal of Mathematic Sociology*, 1, 143–186.

Schelling, T. C. (1978) *Micromotives and Macrobehavior*. New York: Norton.

Schuman, H., Steeh, C., Bobo, L. and Krysan, M. (1997) *Racial Attitudes in America: Trends and Interpretations* (rev. edn). Cambridge, MA: Harvard University Press.

Semyonov, M., Glikman, A. and Krysan, M. (2007) 'Europeans' Preference for Ethnic Residential Homogeneity: Cross-National Analysis of Response to Neighborhood Ethnic Composition', *Social Problems*, 54(4), 434–453.

Sen, A. (2007 [2006]), *Identity & Violence: The Illusion of Destiny*. London: Penguin. 2007 paperback edition.

Small, S. (1994) *Racialized Barriers: The Black Experience in the United States and England*. New York and London: Routledge.

Smith, R. C. (1990) *We Have No Leaders: African Americans in the Post-Civil Rights Era*. Albany, NY: State University of New York Press.

Solomos, J. (1993) *Race and Racism in Britain*. London: Macmillan Press.

Swain, C. M. (1993) *Black Faces, Black Interests: The Representation of African Americans in Congress*. Cambridge, MA: Harvard University Press.

Taeuber, K. E. and Taeuber, A. F. (1964) 'The Negro as an Immigrant Group: Recent Trends in Racial and Ethnic Segregation in Chicago', *American Journal of Sociology*, 69(4), 374–382.

Taeuber, K. E. and Taeuber, A. F. (1965) *Negroes in Cities: Residential Segregation and Neighborhood Change*. Chicago, IL: Aldine Publishing Company.

Taylor, M. C. (1998) 'How White Attitudes Vary with the Racial Composition of Local Populations: Numbers Count', *American Sociological Review*, 63, 512–535.

Taylor, P. and Morin, R. (2008) *Americans Claim to Like Diverse Communities but Do They Really?* Washington, DC: Pew Research Center. Available at: www.pewresearch.org/pubs/1045/

Tomasky, M. (2008) 'How Historic a Victory?', *New York Review of Books*, 55(20). Available at: www.nybooks.com/articles/22156

Ueda, R. (2007) 'Immigration in Global Historical Perspective', in M. C. Waters and R. Ueda with H. Marrow (eds), *The New Americans: A Guide to Immigration since 1965*. Cambridge, MA: Harvard University Press, pp. 14–28.

US Bureau of Census (1943) 1940 Census of the Population, *Subject Reports, Occupational Characteristics*. Washington, DC: US Government Printing Office.

US Bureau of Census (1992) 1990 Census of the Population, Supplementary Reports, 1990-CP-S-1, *Detailed Occupation and Other Characteristics from the EEO File for the United States*. Washington, DC: US Government Printing Office.

Vandell, K. D. (1981) 'The Effects of Racial Composition on Neighborhood Succession', *Urban Studies*, 18(3), 315–333.

Verba, S. and Nie, N. H. (1987) *Participation in America: Political Democracy and Social Equality*. Chicago, IL: University of Chicago Press.

Voltaire (1980 [1734]) *Letters on England*. Harmondsworth: Penguin.

Waters, M. (2009) 'Comparing Immigrant Integration in Britain and the US'. Paper prepared for the Harvard-Manchester Initiative on Social Change. Available at: www.ageofobamabook.com/papers/waters.pdf

Willcox, W. F. (1931) *International Migrations, Vol. II: Interpretations*. Cambridge, MA: National Bureau of Economic Research. Available to download free at: www.nber.org/books/will31-1

Williams, L. F. (1987) 'The 1984 Elections in the South: Racial Polarization and Regional Congruence', in L. W. Moreland, R. P. Steed and T. A. Baker (eds), *Blacks in Southern Politics*. Westport, CT: Praeger Publishers, pp. 77–98.

Winder, R. (2004) *Bloody Foreigners: The Story of Immigration to Britain*. London: Little, Brown.

Wolfinger, R. E. and Rosenstone, S. J. (1980) *Who Votes?* New Haven, CT: Yale University Press.

Wright, T. (ed.) (2000) *The British Political Process: An Introduction*. London: Routledge.

Index